First printing: 2018

Risk Up Front: Managing Projects in a Complex World

ISBN   978-1-54451-086-6   Paperback

         978-1-54451-087-3   Ebook

CELERITY CONSULTING GROUP

2261 Market St #543

San Francisco, CA 94114

www.celerityconsulting.com/riskupfront

Risk Up Front is a registered trademark of Celerity Consulting Group LLC.

Cover Art: Robert Meganck

Illustrations: David Camacho

Names: Josephs, Adam | Rubenstein, Brad.

Title: Risk up front : managing projects in a complex world /

Adam Josephs, Brad Rubenstein

Description: Austin, TX : Lioncrest Publishing, 2018 | Includes index.

Subjects : Project management.

Classification : HD69.P75 R57 2018 | DDC 658.404

LIONCREST
PUBLISHING

MANAGING PROJECTS IN A COMPLEX WORLD

RISK
UP FRONT

ADAM JOSEPHS AND BRAD RUBENSTEIN

CONTENTS

FIGURES

ACKNOWLEDGMENTS

It's a very ancient saying,
But a true and honest thought,
That if you become a teacher,
By your pupils you'll be taught.
— Oscar Hammerstein, *The King and I*

I can no other answer make but thanks,
and thanks, and ever thanks.
— Will Shakespeare, *Twelfth Night*

We want this book to be used. It reflects what we have been taught by the dozens of teams we have had the privilege to work with over the last twenty years. We offer our heartfelt gratitude to our clients around the world. It is through them, with their extraordinary diversity of activities, of skills, of cultures, and of experience, that we have seen what, essentially, makes project teams successful.

We stand on the shoulders of great thought leaders and would like to directly thank those who have taken an interest in our work and guided us: Professor Ron Howard, who taught us the power of the rigorous use of language; Dr. Carol Nash, who demonstrated what impeccable preparation and integrity can accomplish; George Rylander, who is the personification of delivering on big commitments even in the face of circumstances; Cinda Voegtli, who showed us the critical importance of listening and empathy, and the value of a big heart, for masterful project management.

Our ideas would never have made it onto paper without the support and expertise of Dan Bernitt, our editor and project manager. It was a special pleasure working with our illustrator, David Camacho, as well. He was able to take our abstract concepts and translate them into drawings that captured both the detail and the lively spirit that we love to see when our teams "get it."

We want to acknowledge Orion Kopelman and Quality Rapid Product Development for their contributions to the field of accelerated project management.

And finally, to our friends, family, and colleagues who with grace and humor gave their time and energy to push us to complete this book. You have our love, respect, and gratitude.

Adam and Brad

PROLOGUE

A WORLD OF TEAMS AND PROJECTS

Space travel is hard.

December 11, 1998, 18:45:51 UTC: NASA launches the Mars Climate Orbiter from Cape Canaveral. Its mission is to study the climate and atmosphere of the red planet. The orbiter was developed at a cost of $125 million.

September 23, 1999, 09:00:46 UTC: The main engine burn to enter orbit around Mars is initiated.

September 23, 1999, 09:04:52 UTC: Communication with the orbiter is lost. Two days later, the mission is declared a failure.

November 10, 1999: *The Mars Climate Orbiter Mishap Investigation Board [MCO MIB] Phase I Report* is released. In determining how the failure could possibly have happened, the board made some interesting observations:

p. 16:   The MCO MIB has determined that the root cause for the loss of the MCO spacecraft was the failure [by the contractor] to use metric units in the coding of a ground software file...

Lockheed-Martin wrote software using English units while the NASA Jet Propulsion Lab expected metric units. No one noticed, until the spacecraft crashed.

The first recommendation in the report is what you would expect:

> p. 16   The Board recommends that the MPL [MicroPropulsion Laboratory] project verify the consistent use of units throughout the MPL spacecraft design and operation.

The board realized just adding a new item to the design review checklist would not be enough to prevent the next mission failure. In fact, their analysis and recommendations go on for another eighteen pages. We think the board's thoughts are best represented here:

> p. 22   The Board recommends that the MPL project should stress to the project staff that communication is critical and empower team members to forcefully elevate **any** issue;... that they are empowered to **forcefully** and **vigorously** elevate concerns as high as necessary to get attention.... This policy should be **constantly reinforced** as a means for mission success.

The way you prevent the next "unit mismatch disaster" is to establish team norms that result in the early and continuous identification and communication of risks.

This was not a weak team. These were some of the smartest people on the planet. If a team of actual rocket scientists can make this kind of mistake, what hope do the rest of us have? This is what we are up against.

Brilliance, talent, and experience, while certainly useful, do not immunize your project against risks, even obvious ones. And the result is often catastrophic.

This book describes a process for changing the culture and behavior on teams such that they identify and mitigate risks early and often on their projects. Bringing rigor to this activity is at the heart of successful projects.

Over the course of our careers, we've participated in, led, coached, and observed many projects: consumer software projects, industrial manufacturing projects, organizational change initiatives, legislative projects in congressional offices, projects to get the curtain up on theatrical productions, and many more. We've seen projects that are wildly successful and projects that are acknowledged failures.

Many books have been written on how to get teams organized, motivated, and productive. We've seen and used a wide variety of project management strategies, including timelines sketched on a whiteboard, waterfall scheduling, phase gates, Agile/Scrum, Project Management Institute's PMBOK (Google it), "accordion" processes to maximize stakeholder buy-in, lean startup, and so on. Similarly, teams deploy a diverse array of project management tools, including Gantt charts, earned value estimators, kanban boards, integrated continuous development and release management tools, an alphabet soup of software products and cloud services.

Although certain tools and methods are more appropriate for certain types of projects and teams, we repeatedly see projects with first-class tools and methods get into trouble. On the flip side, we've seen complex projects succeed with the barest of project management tools—often no more than a few spreadsheets, lists, and documents.

This book is not about happiness through better Gantt charts.

Most project management books are focused on methodology and tools. They tell you how to press your project through a set of linear or iterative steps. They tell you how to rationally deploy resources or how to calculate a critical path. Do those things, they say, and their process will extrude a successful result.

This book is different. We're going to start by talking about a fundamental shift in perspective that often divides the successful projects and teams from the failures. Then we're going to apply that shift to methods and tools, many of which you already have in place. We are going to introduce an approach that we call Risk Up Front™ (often abbreviated as RUF). It is focused on your team's ability to make and keep commitments by identifying risks early.

HOW TO USE THIS BOOK

In this book, we will show you the Risk Up Front process we use with our own clients and give you the guidance to implement it on your projects. Although it talks about tools and practices, we apply a laser focus to issues that affect behavior and results. In our work, we *develop* high-performance project teams. These teams span many organizational environments; they are often in technology product development. In addition, we work with management to help them create organizations that *foster* the development of high-performance teams. The same core principles we use to upgrade project teams apply to implementing organizational change.

While reading this book, we hope you'll have the aha moment that will make a difference in how you and your team operate. Most of our suggestions may seem to fall squarely in the realm of "common sense." The trick is to make that common sense *more common* in your own actions and those of your teammates. Our clients often describe RUF as a means to scale good project-team practices in an organization. If you find yourself nodding your head in agreement, that's wonderful. But it won't make any difference unless it changes behavior.

As you'll see, creating a common understanding, throughout your team, on how you communicate—what you say, how you listen, and what you measure—is paramount. We expect teams to get rigorous about their communication and language as a requirement for successful project execution and as a prerequisite for using modern project management systems (e.g., Agile, PMBOK, or Lean Startup). To that end, we put forward a set of agreements on what certain words mean. For us, they are bold-faced, reserved words. Although you may have an idea as to what they mean from common usage, we urge you to set aside your preconceptions and use the definitions we provide in sidebars throughout the text. They can also be found in the glossary at the end.

This book is divided into three parts. Part 1 discusses the fundamental dynamics of teams and how this often sets up projects for failure. Risk Up Front offers a different frame to think about what makes teams successful. By the end of part 1, you should have a clear idea of the principles and language of Risk Up Front. You will have a new perspective on how to measure the culture and behavior of your teams.

Part 2 describes, in detail, the critical practices that leverage this new framework to build it into the culture of your organization and teams. The tools and practices discussed in part 2 are appropriate for project teams in all environments.

Part 3 discusses a variety of specific environments where we have experience deploying Risk Up Front. We selected those situations where Risk Up Front has particular benefits or presents particular pitfalls. In each case, you will find a specific description of the use of Risk Up Front in those environments, the pitfalls that teams encounter, and our recommendations for responding to them.

We expect you will read parts 1 and 2 from start to finish. You can then use part 2 as a reference while you're implementing Risk Up Front on your project. You could simply read the section within part 3 that applies to your project environment, but you might be surprised that other environments, seemingly different from your own, may have remarkably similar challenges and benefit from similar risk mitigation strategies.

Refer to the glossary until you are comfortable using RUF terminology with power and precision. The effective use of

Risk Up Front involves the application of a small set of simple practices applied with rigor.

Finally, it's been our experience that the most important thing when introducing a team to these concepts, by your leadership and by your example, is keeping your sense of humor. Enjoy the process. Enjoy the results.

PART 1

PEOPLE, TEAMS, AND WORK

Risk Up Front has a vocabulary of terms that teams need to use clearly, concisely, and quickly.

Many professions and activities depend on specialized terms and definitions in order to perform properly. Mastering these "languages" is critical in fields such as medicine, software development, and construction. This also applies to the subjects of this book: product development, project management, and organizational change.

Throughout the book, we will **highlight** these "reserved words" with their definitions to remind you that when you see or hear them on your projects, we want you to set aside the "common meaning" and understand them in a special way. These definitions are collected in the glossary at the end of the book. Here's the first one:

Project: An activity with a beginning, an end, and a measurable goal.

WHAT IS A PROJECT?

Sometimes, getting out of bed is a project.

We're focused on projects big enough to involve a team of people. Perhaps it's the team that is getting the next version of your test instrument built and into the hands of your customers. Or maybe it is the project to open the factory to manufacture your new computer chip. Or perhaps the project is the delivery of quarterly objectives by the management team. In every instance, there's a beginning, an end, and a measurable goal.

You'd be surprised (or perhaps not) at the answers we hear when we ask teams what they're trying to get done. They describe a stream of activity that has no clear end or that blends all their various and necessary results into an undifferentiated stream of activity. Our first recommendation is always the same—organize a project.

We expect organizations to structure their work into discrete projects, each of which delivers value. Explicitly choosing to shoulder the cost of directing a team to deliver a discrete result, with an explicit value proposition, is basic. In our experience, it is the best way to cause results in an organization.

Do teams engage in "work" that is not project work? Of course. Some do operations, some do maintenance, some do customer support, some do ongoing sales. Sometimes it's helpful to construct these activities as projects; often it's not. The work that supports business processes and workflows is typically outside the realm of projects (however, the work of developing and deploying a new business process could be a project). Whenever you need to organize a team to yield a measurably valuable result by a deadline, seek to organize a distinct project. Give it a crisp beginning, a definite end, and a measurable goal.

We start our discussion of Risk Up Front with how people work collaboratively on teams to get things done. We frame the problem of project management to put team culture front and center.

Chapter 1 analyzes what we consider to be an underlying truth of **projects**—that changes to your project plans become exponentially more expensive as time passes. At the same time, people, particularly when they interact on teams, are designed to procrastinate. To counter this tendency, we introduce the basic principles of Risk Up Front.

The key to our approach lies in how we work with teams to define their projects from the beginning. Chapter 2 walks you through our view of the path a reliable project should take, particularly the conversations about tradeoffs that should occur from the beginning.

At the core of Risk Up Front is the notion of the team's **blind spot** and what teams should do to identify and mitigate risks that lurk there. Chapter 3 discusses what team culture is and how it affects a team's ability to move risks out of their blind spot into a place where the team can get into action. The key to shifting the blind spot is to change your conversations around **risk** and **commitment**.

These changes focus on introducing specific definitions of **accountability**, **transparency**, **integrity**, and **commitment** into your conversations. Chapter 4 captures how we work with teams to understand these principles, show how they affect team behavior on projects for the better, and how to embed these principles into their day-to-day work.

This leads us to chapter 5, on risk. Our practices and structures all rely on a common understanding, throughout the team, of what risk is, how to talk about it, and how to force action in the face of risk. We introduce our vocabulary of risk, based on principles of **cause**, **effect**, and **impact**. Our objective is to mitigate risks early, because that is when change is least expensive.

This lays the groundwork required before diving into part 2, where we will present the structures and practices we teach teams to use. These tools are what allow teams to deliver project results quickly and reliably.

CHAPTER 1

STOP MAKING LATE CHANGES

YOUR PROJECT LIVES ON A CURVE

There has been empirical research since the 1980s that demonstrates a commonsense observation about projects: it's more expensive to make changes late in the project; it is less expensive to make them early in the project. It is less costly in time, resources, materials, and risk to change a mechanical design when it is only on paper than when you have already ordered machined parts, and that is even less costly than needing to make a change after it has shipped to the customer.

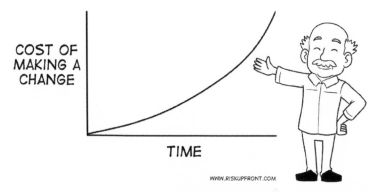

COST OF MAKING A CHANGE

TIME

WWW.RISKUPFRONT.COM

Fig. 1: Your project lives on this curve.

Being on this **cost of making a change** curve is not something that is up to you or your team. It's like gravity: it's there whether you believe in it or not. Even approaches that emphasize responsiveness to changing customer requirements, such as Agile, benefit from activities that reduce the probability of late changes.

Last-minute changes to architecture or performance requirements are all expensive. These costs can arise in the form of money, labor, added risk, market delays, or losing customer trust.

Fig. 2: Late changes are expensive.

Given this curve, it follows that we should avoid expensive late changes. And yet, many projects with talented teams and experienced leaders often find themselves addressing changes late in the game. Just ask the NASA team we introduced in the prologue.

Why does this happen?

PEOPLE ARE OPTIMISTIC PROCRASTINATORS

Consider a simple project that roughly breaks down into three sequential phases:

- Build it.
- Test it.
- Deploy it.

To cover those activities, the team for such a project consists of members from Development, Quality Assurance, and Operations.

The project manager wants to tell management how long this will take, so she builds a schedule. Naturally, she needs to ask, "How long will testing take?" The Quality Assurance team looks at what's being built, and they might create some test plans or testing infrastructure, and so on. The project manager asks the question, "How long will it take?" and after some analysis, she gets an answer, say, "One week."

> **Optimistic procrastination:** The natural, default, human tendency to behave as if everything will go smoothly, and because we're busy now, we'll deal with potential problems and risks later, when we have time.
>
> **Urgency:** The focus, resourcing and issue resolution that is often delayed due to circumstances and **optimistic procrastination.**

However, we know that human beings are optimistic procrastinators. This means the underlying assumption, when you ask them to estimate what's going to happen, is, "If all goes well..." That's the optimism. A sophisticated project manager, aware of this natural tendency, might ask a follow-up question:

"Well, what if all does not go well?" At that point, we often find the team is simply not sure what to say. Who knows what might go wrong? So effectively, the team throws up its hands and says, "We have so many hard things to do right now, we'll cross that bridge when we come to it." That's what we mean by procrastination.

Optimistic procrastination is a consequence of, and exacerbated by, how teams naturally feel urgency on their projects. You may have experienced it this way: A project starts with a few people gathered together, because their manager said, "This seems like an interesting opportunity. What can we build to exploit it?" You brainstorm and bat around some ideas in parallel with all the other work you're doing. It seems worth pursuing, so you draft a rough schedule and notice it's going to involve a few more people, who are not currently available.

Eventually, you add those people, learn more, make some changes, and then build a prototype. People get excited, and a salesperson mentions to a customer it's coming down the pike. Suddenly, the team is being asked, "Can you deliver it sooner and with this one new feature?" One of the team members, now promoted to project manager, does some scheduling to see what it would take and when they can credibly promise to deliver. The team gets to work, with increasing concern as the deadline approaches. Finally, on a death march right before the deadline, the team generates a frenzy of activity and gets it all done, often late. Applause all around.

As in the above example, you can see the urgency of the team typically tracks the **cost of making a change** curve. As the stakes get higher, the team finally learns what it needs to learn, gets the resources it always needed, and makes the hard decisions that should have been made earlier.

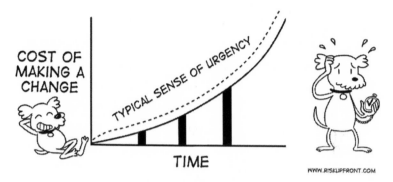

Fig. 3: Urgency typically starts low and increases as deadlines approach.

Delayed urgency and optimistic procrastination go hand in hand. When the deadline is far away, teams feel like they have plenty of time to solve problems later. But this is just an invitation to be thrown off schedule when issues arise late in the project—as they inevitably do.

Our goal is to transform this causal chain where optimistic procrastination and delayed urgency lead teams to defer tough decisions and rigorous risk mitigation, leaving projects derailed by too many late changes.

Risk Up Front is focused on shifting the sense of urgency to the front of the project in order to force issues to be identified and addressed early—when it is less expensive.

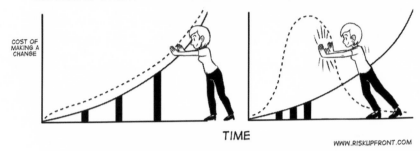

USE **RISK UP FRONT** TO PUSH URGENCY TO THE FRONT OF YOUR PROJECT

COST OF
MAKING A
CHANGE

TIME

WWW.RISKUPFRONT.COM

Fig. 4: RUF shifts urgency to the front; teams identify changes early.

Cost of being late: Pushing urgency to the front of your project is not free. It costs money. You spend this money in order to avoid the substantial costs of missing your schedule or missing your market window.

Making the cost of being late transparent to the team increases urgency and allows the team to make better decisions about how and when they will spend money to accelerate their schedule and mitigate risks.

Your cost of being late is not a single number; It is a narrative describing a set of factors and associated costs. This includes both linear costs (For example, "For every week we are late, we lose $X profit.") and non-linear costs (For example, "If we deliver after date X, we lose customer Y altogether.").

THE COST OF BEING LATE

Why would you expend any effort or behave with any urgency to finish your project at a particular time, or to reduce the likelihood of late changes that jeopardize your promised date, if there were no cost of being late?

In other words, if your project has no cost of being late, why should you bother to be on time?

This may seem like an odd question, because teams often share a "moral" sense that they ought to honor their promises to deliver when they say they will. But with Risk Up Front, we want to make clear our concern is utterly practical. Teams are more productive, and their companies are more profitable, if they *have what it takes* to assess when they will deliver, commit to that date, then finish when they say they will.

Therefore, as part of Risk Up Front, we insist that cross-functional project teams, from the beginning of their project, consider, articulate, discuss, and agree on their cost of being late. It is rarely a single number. Think of it as a set of considerations, with measurable consequences attached. It is, essentially, *the compelling story* that gives the team the incentive to hit their dates. Critically, it creates the context for deciding how much money to spend on ensuring the project completes on time.

Suppose your team is building a product for sale. The product is launched into the marketplace, sales ramp up (and perhaps manufacturing costs stabilize), until a steady state is reached.

Fig. 5: The effect of late delivery on a typical product cycle.

At some point, sales decline, and it may be that sometime later, the product is no longer profitable to sell.

Why does that decline happen? You may have competitors in the marketplace, who come out with a competing product that cuts into your sales. Technology may advance, so your product is no longer competitive. Markets change, customer needs change, and so on.

It is critical for you and your team to understand that the time at which this decline occurs is not under your control. Your customers, your market, and your competition will evolve with or without you.

This means, if you launch your product late, the profit you lose is not simply the cost of moving that whole curve forward in time (the "time cost of money"). The launch ramp is later; the decline is not. The profitability you lose is the lost "steady state"—the most expensive profit to lose.

Let's look at how you answer the question, "What is our cost of being late?" For most projects, it consists of several components, which we can classify as "linear" (costs that accrue day by day) and "nonlinear" (costs, often catastrophic, that hit when a deadline is breached). Here are some linear costs:

- **Lost Profit.** If you are a month late, what is the value of a month of steady-state profit that you will lose over the product's life cycle?

- **Delayed cost savings.** If you are building something that reduces your operating costs, and you deploy it late, what is the value of those foregone savings?

◆ **Additional project expense.** What is the cost of paying the team to work on this project for an additional month?

Often, the nonlinear costs are more important. Here are some examples:

◆ **Breach of contract.** The project delivery date may be written into a contract with your customer. That contract may have specific penalties for late delivery.

◆ **Lost market share.** Even worse than losing a chunk of time at your steady-state profit level, that level may go down as late delivery runs into higher competition or your customers may turn to other solutions to solve their problems. The entire profitability curve will be lower.

◆ **Failure of business processes.** Suppose you are building a system that allows your existing business processes to keep up with your company's growth. If that system is late, at what point do your current systems simply fail? What is the cost to the company of that failure? It could be catastrophic.

◆ **Damage to customer relationships.** What is the value of permanently lost business from a customer who decides, based on your late delivery, that you are an unreliable partner?

◆ **Impact on valuation.** What does the company lose, as its ability to raise financing at favorable terms is degraded? Investors watch the results of the team, as they compare their results to the financial models on which they base their investment decisions.

Fig. 6: The non-linear costs of being late.

The key to making your "cost of being late" useful is to make it measurable. Reduce all the impacts to actual amounts of profit lost or savings forgone. Be accurate where you can, but even a round number or a best guess, widely understood through-out the team, will change the way you deploy resources and mitigate risks.

The practices you put in place when you use Risk Up Front are designed to force a conversation about the cost of being late for your specific project from the start. Involving the entire cross-functional project team in this conversation is important, for two main reasons.

First, in the course of these conversations, the team will discover costs of being late they didn't know they had. For example, the team will discover a customer promise or contract provision they didn't know the company had made, or they may discover that their project is using people whom a later, critical project will need.

Second, the team will finally have a rational way to spend money to reduce risks that impact on-time delivery. For example, we've been in project meetings where a junior engineer *assumes* they don't have time to do a second round of testing on their next-generation software product, and the team discusses how to mitigate that risk. At the tail end of a long meeting, the manager reviews the cost of being late, and the junior engineer then volunteers that buying two additional test machines would allow for the extra testing and mitigate the risk. The manager asked, "Why didn't you suggest that before?" and the engineer replied, "I just assumed management would never approve such a substantial unbudgeted expense, and I would have to live with the equipment we have in the lab. But when I realized the cost of being late was so much larger than the cost of the equipment, requisitioning it was a no-brainer."

HOW DOES RISK UP FRONT WORK?

RUF is, for the most part, indifferent to both the type of product or service being developed and the specific project-management process being deployed. This has allowed RUF to be used in a range of industries, from software to semiconductors to ice machines, and with many methodologies, including Stage Gate, Six Sigma, Agile, and Lean.

Risk Up Front focuses on creating a foundation that allows industry and project-specific tools to be properly leveraged. For example, if a team does not have a foundation in **integrity**, then a project schedule is just one more promise that won't be kept.

Integrity is one of the four principles at the heart of Risk Up Front. These principles live in the conversations of the team, so it is important to define them in language. Here are the core definitions of RUF's four principles:

- ◆ **Accountability:** "Singular ownership of a result."
- ◆ **Transparency:** "Team-wide clarity of what is so."
- ◆ **Integrity:** "Do what you say."
- ◆ **Commitment:** "It will be so, even in the face of circumstances."

You may be thinking these principles are wonderful abstract concepts, but how can we make them show up reliably in practice? Much of the rest of this book is concerned with techniques that take these ideas out of the realm of "aspirational posters on the wall" and engineer them into the day-to-day work of your team.

Risk Up Front depends on four levers to drive change. The four principles are reflected in **language**, because they are concepts that live in the conversations of the team. Another example is the risk language of **cause**, **effect**, and **impact** (CEI) that we use to turn concerns and complaints into action.

Language is one of the four levers Risk Up Front uses to shift behavior and culture. Here are the four levers:

- ◆ **Language,** driving values through conversation;
- ◆ **Structures,** including how you spend money and deploy resources;

- **Practices,** reliably repeated or triggered activities and tools;
- **Metrics,** the results you choose to measure.

These levers make possible many types of changes in an organization's culture, not just Risk Up Front. We will discuss them in depth in chapter 3. Then we will describe in chapter 4 how they allow you to integrate accountability, transparency, integrity, and commitment into your day-to-day work. Chapter 5 then goes into the shift in language for communicating and causing action on risks.

Risk Up Front is different from most methodologies. It is not simply a series of steps or processes. RUF's effectiveness comes from the holistic and ongoing use of these levers *throughout* the project. For example, the full cross-functional project team is deployed to identify hidden risks pervasively, not just at a "risk meeting" in the planning phase.

The tools of Risk Up Front are intended to be used together. The RUF **project statement** looks like a relatively simple project charter document, but when combined with rigorous transparency and the **definition meeting**, it becomes a powerful tool for early risk identification and team commitment. This really is a case where "the whole is greater than the sum of its parts."

If this is sounding a bit poetic, and perhaps confusing, that's OK. We are asking you to make a significant shift in how you think about running projects and creating high-performing teams. The rest of the book will clarify these concepts and discuss how to effectively deploy them on your teams.

CREATING A CULTURE
OF RISK UP FRONT

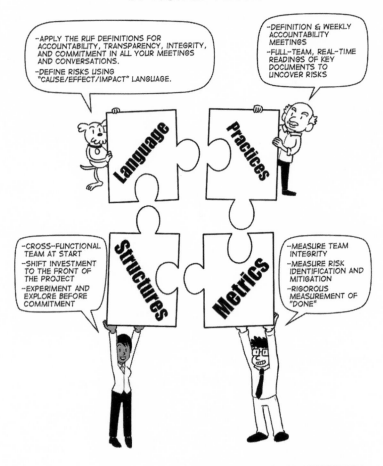

Fig. 7: Creating a culture of Risk Up Front.

Risk Up Front is, ironically, flexible with regard to many of
the classic techniques of project management while being
stubbornly rigorous on certain practices that are not often

explicitly discussed, such as the importance of line-by-line team review of documents and the decisive role of language. Our approach is designed for dynamic organizational environments. Teams are created, then disbanded. Project timelines are short and unforgiving. And teams must anticipate market, technical, and organizational risks. Risk Up Front is a methodology for reliably scaling complex adaptive teams.

You can see the overall picture of what it takes to create and maintain a culture of Risk Up Front on your projects. It is a multifaceted activity. The rest of this book will define each tool to explain how the different pieces fit together. We hope you will enjoy the ride.

THINGS TO REMEMBER

♦ Late changes on projects are expensive, and they cause projects to fail.

♦ People are naturally optimistic procrastinators.

♦ Risk Up Front creates early urgency by increasing accountability, transparency, integrity, and commitment in day-to-day activities.

♦ Implementing Risk Up Front involves making changes to the Language, Structures, Practices, and Metrics within your team and across your organization.

CHAPTER 2

DEFINING PROJECTS IN RISK UP FRONT

THE 5W PROJECT TRADEOFF

From our perspective, there is a critical difference between a project definition and a *committed* project definition. With RUF, teams rigorously work to evolve their project definition into one they can commit to. Only through that process will risks be identified and mitigated, and changes will shift to the front of the schedule.

It is crucial to change the cultural norm on your team from an expectation of "We will do our best!" to the **commitment** "It will be so." This change in perspective affects what goals you choose. For example, you may choose to exclude a feature, because it is risky and thereby hard to commit to. It also affects what you choose to do to achieve those goals. For example, you may proactively fund a backup plan to save your project if some component fails, or you may run a set of experiments "absurdly" early in the schedule to accelerate your understanding of unfamiliar parts of the project.

The classic waterfall of activity that project managers learn is based on a sequence of activities: plan, design, build, test, deploy. But on real projects, this orderly sequence is rarely what happens. When building something, you learn something, so you redesign something, fix your plan, test, learn, and so on. In the real world, we commonly see all these supposedly sequential activities happening in all phases of the project.

Risk Up Front changes the framing. The important thing to do at the beginning isn't planning, per se. Instead, the team will focus on identifying risks of the project. They immediately dive into activities that mitigate those risks, often identifying tradeoffs they can make to arrive at a **project definition** the team can commit to.

THE CLASSIC PROJECT TRADEOFF

Fig. 8: The classic three-way project tradeoff.

The classic project planning tradeoff uses three intertwined dimensions. Typically, these three dimensions are the number of people you bring onto your team ("who"), the number of features you decide to build ("what"), and the amount of time you need to do it ("when"). Because labor is expensive, and customers like features, but budgets are tight, we get the old saying, "You can have it good, fast, or cheap. Pick two."

In this classic world of project management, these tradeoffs serve as a reminder that your decisions have consequences. If you add to the scope of a project, for example, you may need more time or resources. If you want to deliver in less time, you may find yourself reducing the set of features. There's an inevitable push and pull among the three factors that define a project in this model.

In retrospect, it's often easy to see how a failed project broke down along these lines. You might find yourself saying, "The project failed, because the scope was too large given the scheduling constraint." But this three-axis model doesn't suffice for making a robust project definition. It is incomplete.

In RUF, your team will trade off the elements of your project definition along five dimensions.

The axes of our project definition tradeoff are as follows:

♦ **Why:** What commercial opportunity are we intending to exploit? Whom are we doing this project for? Should we satisfy a larger or smaller market segment or customer base?

♦ **What:** What are we going to create to exploit this opportunity? Should we build a bigger thing or a smaller thing?

- **Who:** Who will contribute to getting it done? Who is on the team? Do we need to spend more money? Do we need to add someone with a particular skill?

- **When:** When will it be done? What should change if we need a tighter deadline? What is possible if we give ourselves a bit longer?

- **Why Not:** What risks are we taking on? What is going to be hard? Can we lay off a risk by removing a feature?

For short, we call this the RUF **5W tradeoff**.

THE *RISK UP FRONT* TRADEOFF

Fig. 9: The RUF five-way project tradeoff.

You may be used to starting your project by planning its scope and schedule. Instead, when you use RUF to focus your team on getting clear on all five aspects of your project, you'll find yourself making more honest tradeoffs and uncovering a wider range of risks. Every choice along each axis potentially affects every other one. For example, you can give your team flexibility at the start of your project to adjust the project definition:

- by altering the opportunity you choose to go after and who the target customer will be to fit within the constraints of time and resources or reduce your risks. This may involve adjusting the business case or the resulting value proposition.

- by changing what you choose to build, taking on either more or less risk, as is appropriate for the given value of the opportunity or better matching the resources you have available.

- by modifying who is on your team, given constraints related to budget, availability, and expertise.

- by moving your completion date to consider how quickly your team can deliver. Remember, your schedule must account for the time required to do risk mitigation.

- by altering the risks on your project, adding or removing them, given the experience of your team, the amount of time you have available, what you choose to build, and so on.

Your team might settle on any number of ways in which these elements come together to define a project that is both valuable and achievable. It is a common error to gloss over or ignore the details of the tradeoffs a team is making such that the team ends up defining a project whose tradeoffs don't make sense. For example, once you fully consider the risks, the completion date that had seemed reasonable becomes one you cannot commit to, at least until you make further tradeoffs.

The Commitment Phase

RUF has a name for this process of wrangling your team and your project from a rough opportunity to a project definition that is clear, settled, and committed. We call this phase of your project the **commitment phase**. Most teams begin with, "How should we build it?" In RUF, the **commitment phase** begins with an acknowledgment: "We may not know who the customer *is*, let alone what they want!"

What does it mean to *start* a project? With RUF, the project does not begin *after* you've decided what to do, when you get a team together to build it. It begins *before* you've decided what to do—you need to get a team together to figure that out, because, as you'll see, you will involve the team in determining what the project is. If you don't allow the team to make and own that determination, then there is little room for **commitment**. All you are left with is, "Well, we'll try our best."

The **commitment phase** starts when the project starts. You may have nothing but a rough idea of an opportunity worth pursuing and the name of the **project leader** who's willing to organize a team.

By gathering and focusing a cross-functional **project team** on getting robust **commitment**, RUF creates the urgency required for the team to:

1. focus on the key problem or opportunity, which may not be what they thought,

2. force the early identification and mitigation of risks that stand in their way, and

3. reliably deliver successful project results, on time.

It takes time for a team to work through the ramifications of their choices. Only then should they commit to the successful completion of their project, as defined by its **5W tradeoff**.

To systematically identify risks and focus the team on the tradeoffs they need to make, RUF introduces a series of **definition meetings** during the **commitment phase**. These meetings are messy, exploratory, and expensive. They necessarily involve the cross-functional project team. Project definition can't be done by just a few individuals, because you need to uncover issues and risks encompassing the entirety of the project. Risk Up Front intentionally makes the start of the project slower, more systematic, and more comprehensive, because this is the time when making changes is least expensive.

The **commitment phase** involves real resources, real work, and real time. The decision to initiate a project is precisely the decision to pay for that initial phase. By the time it concludes, the team will have either committed to a **5W tradeoff**, or they will have decided there is no tradeoff that makes sense, and the project should be abandoned.

The risk identification that will transform your projects *emerges* when fully cross-functional project teams rigorously and transparently sort through these difficult tradeoffs.

Perhaps you are used to starting your projects with a "planning" phase. The difference between a "planning" phase and a "commitment" phase is in how you frame your objective. The goal of "planning" is to create a plan. The goal of the **commitment**

phase is to define the project and identify and mitigate risk sufficiently to achieve robust **commitment** to the project definition—tasks extraneous to that goal should be deferred. Now risk mitigation becomes the context for "planning" and other activities. Using this new frame, you wouldn't say you are developing a schedule because it's "good planning," but rather because it would be too risky to commit to a completion date without one.

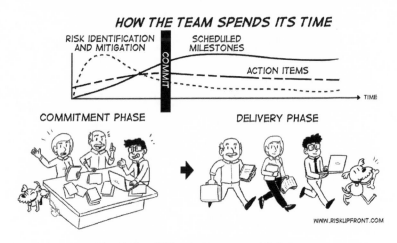

Fig. 10: How RUF project teams spend their time.

We are often asked about the level of detail needed in a schedule. The answer is straightforward: the schedule should be as detailed as necessary to secure the team's **commitment** to the project definition—no more, no less. What does this look like in practice? The team may generate substantial detail in areas that are unfamiliar or otherwise risky. For areas that are well within the core competency of the team, the "planning" could be very light.

What Is Quality?

Teams are often too vague about what constitutes "quality" and what effect different levels of "quality" have on the success or value of their project.

In Risk Up Front, we define quality as the result that achieves customer-perceived satisfaction.

QUALITY = CUSTOMER-PERCEIVED SATISFACTION

Fig. 11: Quality is customer-perceived satisfaction.

This is a baseline requirement for any project. Our rule of thumb is that a satisfied customer is one who "pays the bill and orders more." Your project must achieve a result that satisfies this standard, or you won't meet your commercial goals for the project. You may change the target customer or reduce the features, but you must always deliver a **quality** product or service.

THE ROAD MAP FOR YOUR PROJECT

What does it look like to use Risk Up Front on your project? We'll identify the key points here and go into detail about the various elements in part 2. Remember, words in **boldface** have special, specific meanings in RUF and are defined in the glossary.

Decide to Begin

> **Opportunity:** An idea for a value your team can create, or a need your team can profitably fulfill. The seed of a potential **project**.
>
> **Project leader:** The individual accountable for causing the team to define a committed definition and for causing that definition to be achieved. The project's prime mover.

To begin a project, an organization needs at least two things: an **opportunity** worth exploring and a **project leader** who will lead the charge. The decision to begin the project is a decision by management to spend enough time and money to gather a team and define what the project should be. We haven't decided we're going to deliver any project results yet. At this point, RUF wants the team to assume they don't know what the real problem is or what the solution should be.

Some organizations do lots of planning or have various meetings, or gather stakeholders, or review backlogs to figure out what to do before a decision is made to begin the project. Don't do that. Start the project, *then* do those things.

If your organization runs complex projects with governance/accounting controls, you may have sign-offs that "green-light" the execution of the project, perhaps after presenting the results of various customer analyses and project plans to management or an approval board. Your organization may call that the "start" of the project. To be clear, a RUF project begins earlier and encompasses whatever project planning you do (green-lighting the project occurs in the middle—if the project isn't approved, then the RUF project is simply canceled).

Identify a Cross-Functional Core Team

The **project leader** is responsible for establishing the team for the project. It is "cross-functional," because every aspect of the project that needs to be handled in order for the project to be successful must be identified. Are you deciding who should join your project team as you go along? On a RUF project, you list these individuals by name at the beginning.

> **Core team:** The people in your project team who can speak to "90 percent of the deliverables and 90 percent of the risks and issues" on the project.
>
> We'll describe the structure of RUF teams in more detail, and discuss how to build your project team, including your core team, in part 2.

If you want to identify risks up front, you need the wisdom of the entire cross-functional project team to ensure those risks are raised.

If you're a **project leader**, you need to identify and gather an initial **core team** to begin the process of defining the project. You should aim to get the group of people who can speak to all the areas of opportunity and risk your project will likely cover. Remember, you and the team haven't settled on what your project is, so this first group is almost surely *not* the "right" project team. As the **project definition** is developed and refined, the team will discover who is missing, what areas are under- or over-resourced, and perhaps what new expertise must be hired by the organization. Other people on the initial team list may determine they can't or shouldn't be on the team. Perhaps their priorities are not what the **project leader** thought they were. They will fall off the team. By the end of the **commitment phase**, the team should be complete and settled. The risk that the team might change should be low enough that the team is able to commit to the project.

On smaller projects, the core team may be the entire project team. At a small startup, your core team may be *the entire company*. On larger projects, the structure of the project team is more complex. We will discuss how these more complex teams are built in part 2.

Hold the First Definition Meeting

The goal of the **commitment phase** is to have the **project team** explicitly commit to the right definition (not just *any* definition!) for the project. And by commit, of course, we mean, "It will be so, even in the face of circumstances. You can bet the business on it."

As mentioned previously, the team is not yet certain they have correctly identified the problem to be solved. The first **definition meeting** will begin to identify what is missing. Teams discover they're missing knowledge, missing expertise, missing structure, missing decisions, and taking on risks. Out of this meeting come action items to do research, add talent, set up structures, and mitigate those risks. These actions are what need to happen right away.

The **definition meeting** is run according to a strict agenda. The core activity involves a point-by-point read-through of a document we call the **project statement**. The rigorous read-through is designed to cause the team to uncover issues it was otherwise blind to and get into action on them. It will lead the team urgently toward identifying the issues standing in the way of their **commitment** and make people accountable for resolving them. The focus of this meeting is discovery. The working conversations to resolve any particular nontrivial issue will be done outside this meeting.

What does this meeting produce? Its primary purpose is to identify new risks and action items. These items are entered on a list in the **weekly schedule**, grouped by the week on which they are due. Refining the **project statement** is also important, but your critical objective is to use the meeting to uncover new issues and risks.

The team leaves the meeting with more problems and a lot of work to do. For example, there might be actions related to understanding customer requirements, actions to identify what the scope should be, actions to determine the cost of alternative approaches, and so on. In addition, a critical task is adding items to the **weekly schedule** associated with any new risks that were just uncovered. This is what early urgency looks like.

Initiate the Weekly Accountability Meetings

> **Weekly accountability meeting (WAM):** A weekly meeting of the core team, recurring over the entire time span of the project, designed to measure project integrity, identify risks, and maintain urgency.

The **project leader** is the owner of the **weekly accountability meeting (WAM)**. The **core team** is scheduled to block out one hour per week for the **WAM**, repeating over the entire duration of the project. Even though the agenda typically takes twenty or thirty minutes for many projects, the remainder of the hour is reserved for people to work on issues that are raised in the meeting.

The **WAM** is driven by the **weekly schedule**, and the "week" is defined to span from one **WAM** to the next. Each of the **deliverables** in the **weekly schedule** represents an actual **commitment** ("It will be so!") by its owner to deliver the results of that action item by the due date.

The **WAM** is designed to rapidly accomplish three things:

Make transparent to the full team what percentage of the commitments due this week is, in fact, **done**. We call that the **weekly percent complete**. This pushes the team to measure its **integrity** from the beginning.

Identify (or reconfirm) what the team is committed to deliver by the next **WAM**, adjusting the **weekly schedule**, if necessary, so it transparently reflects that **commitment**. Anything that stands in the way of getting 100 percent complete the next week will be identified and handled.

Each team member will share what she believes to be the "top two" biggest risks to the project. This exercise ensures **transparency**, especially in uncovering risks in habitually overlooked areas of the project.

The **WAM** was developed to replace the long "status meeting," where everyone goes around the room and describes what they are working on, at the end of which no one really knows whether the project is on schedule or not.

Drive the Team toward Commitment to a Definition

The **weekly accountability meetings** continue to pace the team toward resolving the issues that stand in the way of their **commitment** to a project definition. Typically, teams schedule their next **definition meeting** when they have resolved key risks, have made initial meaningful tradeoffs, and have a draft of their schedule. There, the team will again systematically review the **project statement** as it has evolved in response to changes the team has made.

The Moment of Commitment

The core question in all **definition meetings** is, "What stands in the way of our **commitment**?" If the team determines they have handled what they need to handle, they can confidently state their commitment that the project definition "will be so."

Our rule of thumb is a project will need three to five definition meetings spread over the first 25–30 percent of the project timeline to settle the project tradeoff and achieve **commitment**. These meetings are big, long, and often messy.

But essentially, the entire team will be identifying what stands in the way of their **commitment** and identifying and assigning the tasks that will get those things out of their way, who will own them, and by when they will be done. As soon as a **definition meeting** answers yes to the fundamental question regarding their **commitment** to the project, the **commitment phase** is declared complete, and the **delivery phase** begins.

The Delivery Phase

At this point, the **weekly schedule** contains everything the team knows they must complete to deliver the project on time. All that remains is to continue the **weekly accountability meetings** to track that the team is delivering 100 percent of its commitments until they are done.

Will lightning ever strike your project during the **delivery phase**? Of course, it might. For the remainder of the project, the **WAMs** continue polling the team regularly for **risks** uncovered along the way. Even then, the team is getting into action earlier than it would otherwise and making corrections and adjustments to the schedule.

Teams are generally able to handle some number of late fire drills. What breaks projects is when the number or magnitude of the late crises exceeds a workable limit. Risk Up Front, in practice, is successful at reducing the number of late changes. This alone will substantially improve the success rate of your projects.

APPLYING PRINCIPLES TO PROCESS

We have introduced you to the RUF principles for changing how a team assesses project activity and results, and we've described the timeline for how the project will proceed. Let's tie those together.

Filtering your project work through the lenses of **accountability**, **transparency**, **integrity**, and **commitment** orients the team toward actively identifying and mitigating risks early. Without these principles in place, your project can become unworkable. For example, unclear **accountability** might create a team where members don't know what they are on the hook to deliver. Accountable team members will be more likely to identify risks, but without rigorous **transparency**, they will often not share them with their team. Lack of **integrity** may lead to a published schedule that is out of sync with what's happening, and without **commitment**, the team cannot be counted on to deliver as promised.

But that's not the most important issue, and it's not where teams and projects break down. The problem isn't that a team does or does not exhibit **integrity** or **commitment** in what they say and what they do or that they don't want to. It's that they often do not—and cannot—notice when **integrity** or **commitment** are missing.

> **Starting from zero:** Allow your project to start from the point of view that you don't know what you're going to do.
>
> Such a project begins with a group of people representing no accountability (yet), no transparency (yet), no integrity (yet), and no commitment (yet). It is the first priority of the team to recognize that and decide what they will do to address that.

The Risk Up Front approach is designed to cause teams to notice where there is a lack of **transparency**, a gap in **accountability**, a deviation from **integrity**, or an absence of **commitment**.

In fact, a project may start at some moment in time when we don't know what we're going to do, the team hasn't yet been established (we don't know who we need), we don't know what it will take or when we'll finish, and nobody is yet accountable or committed to anything. You may start with nothing more than a single person with an idea or opportunity.

The first tasks of a project are thus related to establishing a team and beginning a **commitment phase**.

THINGS TO REMEMBER

- You need a cross-functional project team to engage in defining your project from the beginning. Your project begins before you know what it is.

- Your team must trade off among five axes to commit to the definition of your project: why, what, when, who, why not.

- Teams must always deliver a quality result. Quality is defined as achieving customer-perceived satisfaction.

- Risk Up Front expects teams to notice and respond when accountability, transparency, integrity, and commitment are missing.

CHAPTER 3

SHIFTING CULTURE:
LANGUAGE, METRICS, STRUCTURES, AND PRACTICES

Consider the entire universe of knowledge, everything a human could possibly know. If we were to ask you, "What is the subset that you know?" you might draw a picture like this:

WHAT YOU KNOW THAT YOU KNOW

Fig. 12: KK—What you know that you know.

What if we were to ask you, "What is the subset of all knowledge that represents things you do *not* know?" You might draw something like this:

WHAT YOU KNOW THAT YOU DON'T KNOW

Fig. 13: KDK—What you know that you don't know.

Suppose you tell me you don't know how to fly an airplane, but you want to. What might you do? Your answers might include "I can read up on flying," "I can take flying lessons," "I can schedule a meeting with a pilot to see what she recommends for how I should learn to fly." When you have a problem, you engage in problem solving.

How does this relate to your projects? Well, teams are good at acting on what they know. Team members often have deep expertise they use every day. When we look closely, we see team members are also good at acting on those things they've identified that they don't know. They solve problems. You can imagine, for example, calling a meeting to discuss and select from among possible solutions to a known issue.

YOUR BLIND SPOT

So if the first slice of the pie represents things you know (and you know that you know them) and the second slice of the pie represents things you don't know (and you know that you don't know them), what is in the rest of your pie?

Blind spot: The things the team doesn't know, and team members don't even know they don't know them. The team cannot act in the face of issues in their blind spot. They cannot make decisions to alter the course of their project.

These are the things you don't know, and you don't know that you don't know them. The things in this part of the pie are in your **blind spot**. These are problems that you have that you don't even know are there. What are you doing to solve them? Nothing. You're not even aware of them.

WHAT TEAMS KNOW AND WHAT THEY DON'T

Fig. 14: DKDK—What you don't know that you don't know.

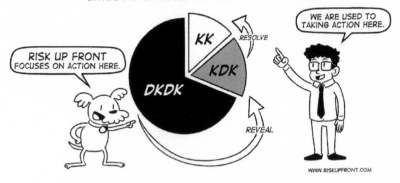

Fig. 15: Invest in uncovering your blind spots.

We will often refer to the space of things "you don't know that you don't know" as the **DKDK**. For example, a meeting to uncover issues in your **blind spot** would be a **DKDK meeting**.

The most dangerous aspect about issues in your **blind spot** is they are outside your ability to act on them. This inability to act is the key feature of a **blind spot**. This contrasts with issues that you are aware of. For example, if you know you don't know how to fly, you may or may not decide to take flying lessons, but at least you have that choice.

This applies not just to you as an individual but also to your team. An individual team member may know about an issue, but if the team isn't talking about it, and the issue isn't being managed by anyone, the team is unable to act. Such an issue is in *the team's* blind spot.

Teams use RUF to uncover these hidden risks. As one of our clients told us, "RUF makes teams constructively paranoid about their ignorance."

Here are some examples that we have seen of teams tripping over their blindspots:

> The hardware team on a manufacturing project has a set of prototypes they need to create. The project manager reviews the schedule for developing the prototypes with the hardware team, and they are committed to deliver them on time. Later, when the work begins, they give their order for the prototype parts to their supply-chain manager, they discover that the lead times are significantly longer than they expected. The prototypes are delivered late, and the entire project schedule is delayed.

What if the supply-chain manager had been in that original scheduling meeting? Even if she didn't have the actual lead times in hand, she might have said, "Perhaps we should check..."

> A software team is building a sophisticated data analysis module for one of their customers. They test the module with sample data, to make sure it is performing properly. Later, as they are integrating the module into the customer's installation, they discover that the customer has key parts of the required input data in different systems, and they have no internal process to get the right data from their global sales force into the system running the data analysis. The team has to stop their work so they can build out and deploy the data collection system. This delays the delivery of the data analysis module.

What if the team had explicitly identified "successful integration" as their measure of success, rather than "delivery of the data analysis module?" This simple change in objective, identified early in the project, might have caused someone to ask, "Where would the final customer data come from?" What if they had confirmed at the beginning of their project what data the customer had locally available, so they could align their analysis to that dataset?

> The project team has a schedule that is posted on the wall of their office. Team members walk past it every day, reading the list of things they need to get done, and the deadlines they need to hit. A few of them notice that certain dates printed on the schedule have already been missed, and are pretty sure that some future dates are in jeopardy. In spite of this, nobody says anything.

Why don't those team members speak up? Are they too busy? Are they reluctant to make waves? Do they assume someone *else* has told the project manager? Perhaps they are saying to themselves, "Since no one else has raised the alarm, it must not be a big deal."

Developing the ability for teams to shine light on their blindspots and take action requires a shift in culture.

WHAT IS CULTURE?

So you stand in front of your team and extol the virtues of **accountability, transparency, integrity**, and **commitment**. You put a motivational poster on the wall. Everyone nods their heads. But nothing changes.

It doesn't work to simply insist on **accountability, transparency, integrity**, and **commitment** on your projects, even if you and the entire team agree "in principle" it would be a wonderful idea. It doesn't change how they act. You can't control or alter how your team members act with respect to

Fig. 16: Motivational posters don't change behavior.

issues in their **blind spot**, issues that they are not aware of. But in fact, teams can act to *shift* their blind spot. It involves a change in culture.

When we talk about "culture" on your team, we're talking specifically about three observable outcomes: **behavior, results,** and **narrative.** Risk Up Front distinguishes four parameters that affect those outcomes: **language, metrics, structures,** and **practices.**

Let's begin by defining these observable outcomes.

Behavior

This is what the individual team members can be observed doing. For example, if five team members show up late to meetings, that is a behavior that can be seen and measured.

INGREDIENTS THAT CHANGE CULTURE

LANGUAGE

NEW TERMS THAT
DRAW DISTINCTIONS,
COMMUNICATE VALUES,
& FOCUS ATTENTION.

EXAMPLES:

- "WE ARE CUSTOMER
  FOCUSED!"
- "WHAT IS YOUR COST
  OF BEING LATE?"
- "INTEGRITY"

METRICS

CHANGE WHAT YOU
MEASURE TO CHANGE
YOUR RESULTS.

EXAMPLES:

- NET PROMOTER SCORE
- DEVICE FAILURES
  REPORTED PER MONTH
- ANNUAL ATTRITION

STRUCTURES

ALLOCATION OF MONEY,
TIME, AND OTHER RESOURCES.
STANDARDIZED USE OF
DOCUMENTS OR BUSINESS
PROCESSES.

EXAMPLES:

- INCREASE TRAINING BUDGET
- PROJECT STATEMENTS
- HIRING THREE MORE
  QUALITY ENGINEERS

PRACTICES

ACTIVITIES THAT ARE RECURRING
OR TRIGGERED WHENEVER A
SPECIFIED EVENT OCCURS.

EXAMPLES:

- PROJECT *WAM* HELD
  EVERY WEDNESDAY
- CODE REVIEW COMPLETED
  BEFORE MERGING
  TO MASTER
- COMPLIANCE TRAINING
  COMPLETED WITHIN TWO
  WEEKS OF EMPLOYEE
  START DATE

WWW.RISKUPFRONT.COM

Fig. 17: The cauldron of culture.

Results

This is what happens with regard to objectives, "What is so." "Revenues from sales" are a result. Completing a project by a deadline is a result. Completing a project *after* a deadline is also a result.

Narrative

These are the stories and explanations team members tell one another about what's happening, about their results and behavior. It is the interpretation of observations. It is mental model development, myth making, and sense making. Narratives are how people inevitably explain, evaluate, compare, assess, and judge both behavior and results. In our example, the other meeting attendees might complain that meetings are not important. Or they might tell one another, "Tardiness is completely understandable. Nobody arrives to meetings on time. How could we, given how chaotic the office is?"

HOW TO ENGINEER TEAM CULTURE

Managers, consultants, and team members would love to change these aspects of culture directly. Unfortunately, this usually does not work. A company-wide email or a speech at the employee meeting is not enough to change culture. We want you to think of behavior, results, and narrative as *dependent* variables. You must leverage indirect approaches that alter behavior. In RUF, we suggest the following four *independent* variables—**language**, **metrics**, **structures**, and **practices**. Think of them as dials on your cultural control panel you can turn directly.

Language

The act of introducing new language, new jargon, or new terminology can change how teams frame and communicate issues. For example, teams that don't have the term *released to production* may be confused whether a piece of software code is, in fact, done. Another example: by training a team to use precise language to articulate risks, they change not only what risks get identified but also their ability to get into action to mitigate those risks. Language is also how you declare the values that are important to your team, such as **integrity** and **transparency**. These may take the form of company policies, principles, or mission statements. Consider how the language in these statements influences the conversations on your team. For example, ambiguity in your policies may be creating **blind spots** and confusion.

Metrics

It's often said, "You don't get what you want; you get what you specify." In our experience, this isn't correct. You don't get what you specify; you get what you *measure*. When you want to change your results, start by getting rigorous about measurement.

Good metrics are meaningful, measurable, and manageable. What you choose to measure will define where your team focuses. For example, a company may decide to measure customer satisfaction scores. They know this will orient the attention of the team toward satisfying their customers. Changes in behavior come from making those scores transparent to the organization.

What you measure impacts the culture and tells the team what is important.

Structures

Structures exist in time and space and require resources (usually money). They can be specific to a project—for example, a testing lab that supports a test plan. They can also be organizational structures, such as a new department with appropriate budget.

Organizations can affect behavior, results, and narrative by changing their structures—for example, adding more vacation days for employees or hiring shuttle buses between San Francisco and Mountain View. Adding and changing structures in an organization involves decisions that allocate capital (physical resources, human resources, or money).

People naturally "follow the money." Team members notice how management allocates money and other resources to tell what the organization values. Spending money consistent with declared objectives nudges the culture in that direction.

Practices

Practices are the activities the team engages in periodically and systematically. A team that decides it is their practice to have a weekly team meeting never finds itself asking, "Do we need to have one this week?" It's a practice. They just do it. Some practices aren't periodic but triggered by some occurrence. For example, a hardware team decides it's their practice to conduct a design review every time a circuit board has been revised. They don't argue; they just do it. A common type of practice is a meeting with an established fixed agenda. In RUF, the **definition meeting** and **weekly accountability meeting** are practices.

The "just do it" aspect of practices is the key to removing **blind spots**. Consider code reviews. If you only schedule a code review when you discover and fix a bug in a code library, you risk that your code library will still contain bugs because of things you didn't know you didn't know. To mitigate this risk, you would identify whether a library is "critical" and rigorously schedule a code review every time any critical library changes.

Practices also involve the development, maintenance, and communication of documents. For example, a team may have the practice of getting a design specification reviewed and approved by a design review board before it may be implemented. RUF has specific **project documents** that, when used in a rigorous way, change behavior and move **blind spots**. For example, the very fact that the RUF **weekly schedule** is a table with an "owner" column *unblinds* the team to the risk that an action item doesn't have a person accountable for delivering it. Teams transition their language from "It didn't even occur to us that this thing would fall on the floor for lack of an owner" to "This thing has no owner; let's fix that now." Action items required for the success of the project reliably get associated with owners whom the team can count on to deliver them. Deliverables fall through the cracks less often.

Bringing It Together

In summary, it is useful to think of your team culture as simply the totality of their **behavior**, the **results** they generate, and the **narrative** meanings they attach to their results and behavior. To change culture, Risk Up Front introduces new language, new metrics, new structures, and new practices.

Fig. 18: Four levers for engineering organizational culture.

When we talk about these concepts with teams, one of our goals is to change their culture in ways that will make them "risk-identifying machines." Simply introducing these terms into their working vocabulary causes these kinds of changes:

- Once they get that "language changes culture," they ask questions such as, "Can we get more of this behavior by naming it?" An example of this could be, "Can we reduce the risks of unexpected warranty costs by naming a set of activities 'Design for Reliability'?"

- Once they get that "metrics change culture," they ask questions such as, "How will we measure that?" Or they stop obsessively optimizing code (it happens) because the team has stated how fast the code needs to be, and when it's fast enough, they can declare the resulting code complete, and move on.

- Once they get that "structures change culture," they will insist on getting the resources they require to mitigate high risks to create a culture of **commitment**.

- Once they get that "practices change culture," teams realize that their **weekly accountability meetings** generate a rhythm that creates urgency on their projects, and their narratives about their ability to get things done change significantly as they see their **weekly percent complete** at 100 percent each week.

An Example: Better Meetings

During our assessment interviews with one of our clients, we kept hearing persistent complaints about their meetings.

> "There are too many meetings."
>
> "We can never start on time."
>
> "We can't get anything done in meetings."
>
> "The loudest voices commandeer the agenda, and our meetings go off the rails."

The team was clear they wanted to change their culture around meetings, and so we asked them to describe, "What would the world look like if you were having great meetings?" When we had them break it down into behavior, results, and narrative and asked them to be specific and measurable, they wrote this on their whiteboard:

- ◆ **Behavior:** Over 80 percent of our meetings start on time.

- ◆ **Results:** We spend 10 percent less time in meetings than we do now. Projects finish sooner than currently targeted.

- ◆ **Narrative:** Team members will find themselves saying things to one another that reflect their perception that meetings work, such as, "We start meetings on time," "We don't waste unnecessary time in meetings."

The next step was to determine how they would move the levers of culture. They got creative and came up with these ideas (among many others):

- **Language:** We'll define and talk about "meeting integrity." If integrity is "doing what you say" (chapter 4), "meeting integrity" applies to meetings that accomplish what they were scheduled to accomplish.

- **Metrics:** Fraction of meetings that start within five minutes of their scheduled start time.

- **Practices:** For every meeting that has an Outlook meeting request, attach a goal and an agenda to the meeting invitation. Talk about "meeting integrity" in the training session for new employees.

- **Structures:** Deliver an "effective meetings" course. Train project teams on how to organize and execute effective meetings. Identify professional meeting facilitators to be available for important, complex meetings.

These are just examples, the team realized there was no silver bullet for fixing their culture—they attacked the problem from many angles. The key was to make creative use of all the levers they had available. Excellent meetings are such an important part of Risk Up Front practices; we have a lot more to say about them (see chapter 6).

Another Example—Improving Customer Satisfaction

In a different company, there was serious concern about the severity and frequency of customer complaints and dissatisfaction with their customer support process. Both the customer service team and their management were involved in figuring out how to remedy this.

Again, we asked them to describe, specifically and measurably, "What would the world look like where your customer service is excellent? What would show up?" Here are a few examples from their answers:

◆ **Behavior:** Customer support calls are returned within twenty-four hours.

◆ **Results:** The "New Promoter" score on our customer satisfaction survey is 10 percent higher than it is now. Customer turnover at year-end is 15 percent lower than last year.

◆ **Narrative:** The conversation within the company, and among our customers, reflects statements such as, "We take care of our customers" and "We take customer support seriously."

Here are some examples of decisions the team made in how they would change their culture around customer support:

◆ **Language:** When assessing the impact of product and resourcing decisions, we'll address how they impact our "focus on the customer." We'll talk publicly about "world-class customer support," with evidence from our performance metrics and customer surveys to back it up.

◆ **Metrics:** Measure response time to customer escalation and reduce it by 10 percent. Track escalation close rate. Track "Net Promoter" score.

◆ **Practices:** Survey Tier 1 customers every quarter. Management reviews escalation list and response time as a fixed agenda item of their monthly management meetings. Review and upgrade our support process every quarter.

♦ **Structures:** Deliver customer support training. Reward excellent customer support. Increase customer support resources to deliver on support objectives.

Again, these are only a few of the changes this team chose to put in place, but we want you to observe the level of specificity in their decisions. They were able to set up a process against which they could transparently measure whether they were succeeding or not, and make adjustments accordingly.

THINGS TO REMEMBER

♦ People naturally spend their time and resources focusing on things they "know" and things they "know they don't know." But the issues in their **blind spot** (things they don't even know they don't know) are the most dangerous.

♦ The problem with issues in your **blind spot** is you are *unable to act on, or even discuss*, these issues, because they are invisible.

♦ Your culture is a result of the **language, metrics, structures**, and **practices** you choose.

♦ Risk Up Front uses these four levers to create a culture that focuses obsessively on moving your **blind spot** to identify risks early.

CHAPTER 4

THE FOUR PRINCIPLES OF EFFECTIVE TEAMS

Let's circle back and tell a more complete story about the core principles underlying Risk Up Front. Knowing what we now know about culture, let's see how we frame them to upgrade your team's behavior, results, and narrative.

ACCOUNTABILITY

Let's start by making the connection between **accountability** and results. It should be obvious it's more likely something will get done if someone has agreed to get it done. Yet, it's surprising how often we hear teams say, "Someone really needs to do X," and then they let it drop. Team members get shy about forcing the team to make sure there is a name attached to any activity that the project wants to get done. Assigning a task to a department is inadequate. Things change when teams root themselves in **accountability** as a core principle, in language and in practice.

Of course, all teams realize it takes more than just assigning people to do stuff. RUF has a specific definition of

accountability—singular ownership of a result. This requires that everything that needs to get done has an accountable **owner**, and every accountable owner is committed to doing what she said she will do.

Risk Up Front has a specific technique for establishing **individual accountabilities** on a project. By engaging each team member in generating her own individual accountabilities, the team will reduce the risk that responsibilities will be attached to people without their being aware of it (no more "I didn't know that was my problem"). Observe that the process for generating and approving each member's **individual accountabilities** is a **practice**, triggered by the start of the project, or when a team member joins. It's a "just do it" ritual. It works when kept in **integrity**.

Ownership Is a Causal Role

In RUF, we insist the assignment of owners be complete—no unowned action items. Before writing down the name of a team member as owning an action item, that individual must agree to take responsibility for it. Do not assign an item to a person who is not in the room. Only an individual can accept accountability, not a functional group. Assign accountability to people by name, not by their job titles. The process of asking for consent when assigning ownership and handling the resulting yes or no is an important part of any meeting.

Just because you are accountable for a result does not necessarily imply that you will do any of the work (although you might). You're accountable for causing it. That means, for example, if you can't do it, you're on the hook to find someone who can. If you are on the hook to solve a problem, and that requires a meeting, you will cause the meeting to be scheduled where people come together to solve the problem.

Avoiding "Project Democracy"

We don't want decisions on a project to be made by consensus. When we see this "project democracy," we suspect the team is unwilling to hold individuals accountable or doesn't trust individuals to make good decisions. This slows projects down and often makes them unworkable.

> **Result:** A specific, measurable outcome to be achieved by a deadline. Inarguably done or not done.
>
> **Owner:** The team member on the hook to cause a **result**.
>
> **Decision:** A transparent choice to allocate resources to achieve a result.
>
> **Action:** Behavior and activity on the team that leads to **results**. Tasks.
>
> **Measurable:** A result is measurable when you have both identified what will be measured and decided what measured value represents success.

If the team doesn't trust an accountable owner to make the right decision in their area of **accountability**—drawing on whatever expertise, research, stakeholder feedback, and team wisdom that the owner feels they need to gather to make the decision properly—then that owner is the wrong person for the job. Of course, a **project leader** can set ground rules that constrain what decisions team members make. For example, the system architect on your team may be accountable for deciding on the system architecture, but that doesn't mean the organization can't require sign-off from a review committee before making their decision.

It's critical to decouple the question of who should make the decision from the decision itself. Settle **accountability** early in the **commitment phase** so you're not fighting over "Whose call is it?" and "What should the decision be?" in the heat of mid-project decision making.

Ground Rules

Organizations, over time, often develop rules, governance standards, and cultural norms (Structures, Practices, Language, and Metrics) that we can think of as baseline accountabilities that apply to any team member who fills a role. For example, "If I've committed to attend a meeting, I'm accountable for arriving on time," is often an interesting ground rule. A more specific example is a software organization that might say, "Software developers are accountable for developing, committing, and running unit tests alongside all software that will be released into production."

If you're starting a new organization, consider having the team members, as they design their individual accountabilities, think about what accountabilities should be adopted by the entire team to "set the standard" for their work.

TRANSPARENCY

The moment an individual speaks up and says she will be accountable for a result, she has a problem. How does she know what the result should be? What if the result she agrees to is not the result that's needed? What if the result she agrees to isn't the result the team asked for? These misunderstandings are common and often fatal to the success of projects. To address this, RUF insists that teams get rigorous about noticing failures of **transparency**.

Transparent Measures

We need to be rigorous about our language in the **project documents**. For example, in the **project statement**, each of the **customer measures of success** must be necessary and sufficient for the success of the project. The fact that they are in the project statement means the team has made that decision. In addition, at the end of the project, the team must demonstrate those measures were achieved.

Consider the practice of the **definition meeting**. During that meeting, the team does a ritualized read-through of the items in the **project statement**. Team members are asked if the language expressing each item is clear enough that members *really do agree* on what that item means. By forcing these questions to be addressed during the **commitment phase**, the team is less likely to be blindsided by risks stemming from ambiguous language late in the project.

Conversations Disappear: Write Things Down

The most common improvement we see teams make in their behavior, in the name of **transparency**, is they write down their decisions on documents that are actively reviewed. Only then will teams notice and fix the descriptions of the results they need, wherever they are ambiguous and unclear. They'll do so early in the project, while team members are making tradeoffs to arrive at **commitment**, rather than later during the delivery phase when the ambiguity resurfaces in the form of a disaster.

What does it look like when teams focus on **transparency**? In a project team meeting, we expect to see conversations like this:

> **Project leader, Katja:** Raul, what's your deliverable for next week?
>
> **Raul:** I'll code up the translation module.
>
> **Katja:** Let's focus on the deliverable—how will we know it's done?
>
> **Raul:** The code will be checked into the repository, along with its unit tests that confirm it matches the spec we approved.
>
> **Katja:** So the deliverable is a complete translation module? (Katja writes down the action item: Translation module complete, unit-tested to spec, committed to repo. Owner is Raul. Due Tuesday.)
>
> **Irfan:** Does that include the web interface?
>
> **Raul:** No, just the back-end API.
>
> **Katja:** (Erases what she wrote, writes, Translation module back-end API complete, unit-tested to spec, committed to repo. Owner is Raul. Due Tuesday.)
>
> **Belinda:** Will the code review have been done by then?
>
> **Raul:** I didn't think about that, but of course we have to. If we're going to schedule and hold that meeting, we can commit to being done by the following week.

Katja: (With a smile on her face, erases what she wrote: Translation module back-end API complete, unit-tested to spec, committed to repo, reviewed. Owner is Raul. Due Tuesday after next.)

Katja, to the room: (Reads what she wrote) Is that clear? Is it correct?

Raul: Yes!

Irfan: Yes!

Belinda: Yes!

When a team is committed to rigorous **transparency**, this is what it looks like. Take a moment and reread this little dialogue and identify the potential misunderstandings that the team avoided by having the above conversation. Notice how Katja, as **project leader**, takes a stand that deliverables be written down using language that is clear, complete, specific, and measurable. She keeps her ears open for language that is ripe for misunderstanding and insists other team members do the same.

When teams first insist on this level of transparency, there is a lot of erasing in their meetings as they notice where they lack clarity and what they need to fix. But after a short time, team members become competent at describing their deliverables clearly from the start. In addition to reducing project risk, they find that recording high-quality, transparent action items goes much faster.

INTEGRITY

While **transparency** obligates the team to make a reliable connection between what is meant with what is said, **integrity** insists the team draw the connection between what is said and what is done. In fact, reducing the amount of time wasted on confusion about what is done and what is not done is an important consequence of a rigorous commitment to **integrity**.

You Get What You Measure

"Knowing where you are" is critical to achieve a goal. It has been shown that starting to measure a given activity will often improve results.

> It is lunchtime at a Risk Up Front workshop in the Netherlands. We let the thirty participants know the break will be an hour long and ask, "Will everyone be back in their seats by 1:30 p.m.?" Everyone nods. We then ask explicitly if anyone will not be back in one hour. No one raises their hand. Clearly, everyone is on board with the time and schedule.
>
> At 1:31 p.m., we count the participants who are back in the room. There are twenty-one of the thirty participants ready to go, and we note this on the whiteboard: *21 delivered out of the 30 who committed*. In the workshop, we spent considerable time discussing integrity, yet only 70 percent of those who committed to return did what they said they were going to do.
>
> The participants weren't happy that we were counting. It took time and discussion to become comfortable with the fact that when they said something would happen, we would account for whether it happened or not, transparently. Counting measured the

integrity. At the end of the day, we asked if anyone was unable to be in their seats in the morning at 9:00 a.m., and at 9:00 a.m. the next day, we counted. Every seat was filled, and we recorded 100 percent integrity between what the group committed to be so and what was so.

We see this all the time. The simple act of transparently accounting for results *improves results.*

Managing for Integrity

Katja (two weeks later, in a room with Raul, before the WAM): Is our translation module back-end API complete, unit-tested to spec, committed to repo, and reviewed?

Raul: (Tells a very long story about which parts are done, a few parts where they got stuck, but we're nearly there, and as soon as those get resolved, we can check the code in—the unit tests are ready to go and won't take long.)

Katja: So "not done"?

Raul: Correct.

Katja: What do we need to do to keep our commitment to the project definition?

Raul: Irfan can do the accounting web UI this week instead of next, so we can finish the translation back end, and he can then begin its UI. We'll still be able to complete successfully on time. I can commit to delivering the completed translation back end by next WAM.

Katja: Does anything stand in the way of keeping our commitment to the project definition as it is?

> **Raul:** Let me check with Irfan first.
>
> **Katja:** Thanks. Please confirm your and Irfan's commitment, given your adjustments, before the next WAM.
>
> **Raul:** Will do!

This is what a **commitment** to **integrity** looks like, in noticing clearly what is done and not done. It also shows what it looks like to notice where a breakdown in **integrity** occurs and how it can be straightforwardly fixed. Except for Raul's long story (which, he admitted later, was completely unnecessary), the entire conversation identified a need to reconfirm the **integrity** of the schedule and put in action the plan to rapidly do so, easily.

Notice Katja and Raul were able to recover the schedule quickly because they and the team had a shared and settled **project statement**. Even though that document is frozen when the team exits the **commitment phase**, it is used actively for the remainder of the project as the map against which changes will be measured. This works for all the **project document** structures, because we are explicit about what types of claims each project document must cover.

Apply Integrity to Commitments, Not People

People may race to the judgment, "Having **integrity** is good; not having **integrity** is bad." In fact, you may be used to saying things like, "This person has **integrity**; that other one, not so much." That isn't RUF. For our purposes, **integrity** is not about an individual; it's about specific instances of language and results. Was a commitment made, and was it kept?

RUF fully expects that the **project documents**, at the early stages of the **commitment phase**, will be full of statements that are placeholders, untested hypotheses, misunderstandings, and outright mistakes. This is normal. As you are reviewing and clarifying those statements, ask yourself if you will be able to test whether they are so. If your commitments are unclear or untestable, then the team will find itself arguing later about whether stuff is done or not.

COMMITMENT

Upgrading a team's conversations around **commitment** can improve the reliability of its projects, as seen in this exchange:

> **Katja** (on Tuesday): Raul, can you get me the spec for the translation module by Thursday morning?
>
> **Raul:** Sure!
>
> **Katja:** Thanks!
>
> (Thursday arrives.)
>
> **Katja:** Raul, I didn't see the translation module spec. Did you send it?
>
> **Raul:** Oh, sorry. I needed to include the interface points from Belinda, and she had to fly to Japan to help the Tokyo team yesterday. I'm pretty sure I can get it to you by next Tuesday.
>
> **Katja:** Um...OK. (Smiles wanly)

What might this look like if Katja and Raul had decided they would aim to upgrade their ability to get things done by making clear commitments, where they both define **commitment** as "It will be so, even in the face of circumstances"?

> **Katja** (on Tuesday): Raul, will you commit to getting me the spec for the translation module by Thursday morning? What might stand in your way?
>
> **Raul:** (Stops and thinks about it) I think so, but I can't commit. I'll need the interface points from Belinda, but she can probably get them to me tomorrow. So Thursday shouldn't be a problem.
>
> **Katja:** Can you confirm that?
>
> **Raul:** I'll give her a call now and let you know in half an hour.
>
> **Raul** (half an hour later on Tuesday): Katja, it turns out Belinda has to deal with a fire drill on the Tokyo team, but she can get me the information on Thursday, and I will commit to getting you the spec on Friday.
>
> **Katja:** Great, I can make that work on my side. Thanks for letting me know!
>
> **Raul:** I'm glad we were able to deal with this today and not on Thursday when it would have been too late! [He didn't actually say that, but we added it just to make the point clear.]

This is how conversations between team members change, when they agree to upgrade their commitment from "I'll try" or "I'll do my best" to "It will be so!" It causes teams to communicate and get into action on the things that stand in their way. Notice it takes both people to make this work: Katja, instead of casually saying what she needs, explicitly asks for Raul's **commitment**; Raul, understanding **commitment** means something special, stops to determine if he can make it so and handle whatever might come up. That causes him to realize he has a dependency on Belinda, and he needs to secure her **commitment** before he can give his.

Insisting on integrity and commitment in this way results in risks being reported earlier, in both project discussions and in day-to-day conversations. This represents a transformation in team culture and leads to greater project success.

The Paradox of Commitment

A paradox has two sides that contradict each other. On the one side of the **commitment** paradox, we are asking you to use this upgraded definition of **commitment**: "It will be so!" On the other side, the simple reality is that you will not keep every **commitment** you make in your life.

We are advocating, even in the face of this paradox, that you use the upgraded definition of **commitment**.

We staunchly believe in this approach for two reasons. First, making high-quality commitments yields real results, even if some commitments are not met. Second, creating a culture of upgraded commitments leads to earlier risk identification. In practice, when teams take their commitments seriously, they will be more judicious in what they commit to and will be more communicative and proactive in identifying and mitigating risks.

When we ask team members to commit to deliver a result, they often say, "How can I possibly commit? There are surely things that might happen that I can't handle. What if there's an earthquake? What if I break my leg?" But consider you do this all the time. Here's an example:

> **Mary:** Honey, can you pick up little Rasheed at nursery school today?
>
> **Umesh:** Sure, honey.

Umesh is probably not relating to that response as, "Well, I'll do it if it is convenient, but if something comes up, no big deal." It turns out that after lunch, Umesh gets into a fender bender, a minor car accident.

Now, he could take a taxi home that evening, and perhaps this is how the conversation would then continue:

> **Mary:** Um, honey, where's Rasheed?
>
> **Umesh:** Oh, it's terrible. I got rear-ended after lunch, and it totally smashed the fender of the Prius, and I had to take it to the shop, so I couldn't get to the nursery school. Oops.

But of course, that's not at all what he said. Instead, he realized he'd committed to his wife he'd pick up their son. When the problem came up, he immediately called his wife.

> **Umesh:** Honey, the car got rear-ended, and it's being taken to the shop. I'm fine, but I can't get to the nursery school in time. What will we do?

> **Mary:** The Prius? You wrecked the Prius? Goodness! [Pause] Call Katja and see if she can fetch little Rasheed when she picks up her own daughter. I can stop by her place this afternoon and pick him up there.

The point is, when it really matters, you do make commitments. If something arises that gets in your way, you immediately respond to it with seriousness and the expectation that you'll work to figure out the best way to respond. That's how you want your team to behave.

Human beings make promises. Sometimes they keep their word; sometimes they break their word. That's what humans do. But teams that make commitments with seriousness and rigor, even knowing the universe is cruel and sometimes they'll fail, make them anyway knowing they'll improve their results by doing so. This is a muscle you want your teams to develop.

Managing for Commitment

If you are a manager or **project leader**, and you need something to happen, be sure to identify an accountable owner on your team to cause it to happen. Then explicitly ask her for her **commitment** to get it done by a deadline. This is true for both big things and small things. Remember:

> Action = Clear Measurable Result
>
> + Committed Owner
>
> + Deadline Date
>
> + Written Down

Accountable owners may want to say yes and say it immediately. Don't let them. Remind them you want the **commitment** to mean it will be handled, regardless of circumstances, and then ask questions like these:

- Do we agree what "done" means? What can we do now to avoid arguing on the deadline date, whether it's done or not? What would we be arguing about?

- What might prevent the result from being delivered completely by the deadline?

- Does the result depend on anything that's not currently under your control?

- Is there anyone you need to check with to confirm that it will be so?

- Is there anything you need me to get out of your way for you to deliver the result by the deadline date?

To avoid common breakdowns in getting **commitment** from your team, focus on getting these things right:

- **Write them down.** The typical place to write down most of the week-to-week commitments is in the **weekly schedule**. But this points to a general principle: never rely on spoken conversations for commitments. Unless they get written down, you won't be able to track, hold people accountable, or measure your team members' performance with respect to their commitments.

♦ **Ask for commitment to results that are valuable.** Avoid managing and tracking things that are straightforward, low risk, or low value. Focus on the valuable result, not the tasks or activities that get you there. Trust owners to engage in whatever activity they must so long as the results are achieved. For example, if the risk is your transceiver won't be fast enough, perhaps you don't need to commit to "design the transceiver"; rather, you should commit to "run a simulation on the transceiver design to confirm it conforms to its specification; email the results to the team." In this example, designing the transceiver is just one of the steps to get you to the valuable result—a transceiver that is fast enough.

♦ **Word your commitments so the "done/not done" outcome will not be arguable.** As you write things down, include in the results the key end points that make them valuable. For example, don't write down, "Prepare XYZ report." Instead, write, "XYZ report submitted to document repository and emailed to team." Notice, as stated, it will be inarguable whether this is "done" or "not done." That's how you know the result is clear and measurable.

♦ **Negotiate commitment.** You must be willing to accept a "no," not as the end of the conversation but as the beginning of a negotiation. If there's no room for a "no," then a "yes" is meaningless. If you find yourself saying no, share the blocking issue, and make a counterproposal then and there—you may quickly discover a way around your roadblock.

- **Make room for risks.** Your team needs to understand that exploring reasons why something will fail is a positive thing. Teams are often afraid to bring up reasons something will fail. Explicitly insist your teams step up and do it.

- **Insist on action.** Don't let risks languish as complaints or excuses. Use **CEI form** (see chapter 5) to focus teams on mitigating those risks. The amount of mitigation you need is just enough so the owner is able to commit ("It will be so!") to deliver the required result—no more, no less.

THINGS TO REMEMBER

- Use Risk Up Front language with precision. It allows your team to establish **accountability**, **transparency**, **integrity**, and **commitment** with rigor and consistency from the beginning.

- There can be only one accountable owner for any given result or decision.

- **Transparency** requires overcommunicating information and decisions on your projects.

- You must be able to measure **integrity** for it to be useful.

- When asking for **commitment**, if there is no room for "no," then "yes" is meaningless.

CHAPTER 5

THE LANGUAGE OF RISK

We now turn our attention to the specific language teams use to talk about risk.

Remember, people are "optimistic procrastinators." If I have a concern about something that might be a problem, but I'm not sure it will be a problem, why would I bring it up? The team might consider me to be pessimistic, impolite, confrontational, or "a complainer." If I raise concerns about issues in my own area of responsibility, the team may think I'm not up to the job. (If I were, I'd "just deal with it.") If I raise concerns I notice in someone else's area, other team members may get defensive and not be willing to work with me. If this is the dynamic on your team, how do you talk about risk? You don't.

Without specific training, focus, and rituals that make risk conversations constructive and necessary, teams have a tremendous bias against having any risk conversations at all.

The other dynamic we see, especially among teams that know they need to talk about risk but don't know how to do it productively, is they squawk at one another. Their fundamental unit of risk conversation is the "complaint." You've heard team members, perhaps even yourself, say things like:

> "There's nothing we can do about it."
>
> "It's not my job."
>
> "They'll never change."
>
> "No one wants to hear it."
>
> "Risks are all surprises."
>
> "They'll take it as criticism."
>
> "I'm already doing everything I can."

We work with teams from various cultural and language backgrounds, and they never have any problem sharing with us their own list (in their own language) of complaints they hear over and over, like a broken record.

This shows up not only in how people talk about their risks but also in how they listen to team members identifying risks. The presumption that risks are complaints leads you to shut down your listening. To make risk conversations productive, we need to address both how teams talk and how they listen.

These habits calcify within teams and within organizations, shutting down those conversations about risk that contribute to the success of projects. To alter these dynamics and change team culture, we focus obsessively on language. We train teams to describe their risks using a specific language game, and this change in how teams speak and how they listen to this language increases the likelihood there will be real action to mitigate risks.

> Suppose I say to you, "I'm worried that I'll get into a car accident on my way home from work."
>
> What might you say to me in response?
>
> You might say, "I'm so sorry to hear that," or "Well, I certainly hope not," or, "Drive carefully!"

This is a common way we talk about risks—we describe a future bad outcome. Perhaps you've heard team members say, "The design won't work," "The schedule will slip," or, "We won't hit our cost targets." These are the worries that keep teams up at night. In Risk Up Front, we call these statements the **effect**, which we define as "a possible future bad outcome."

But notice your beliefs about the future are rooted in your assessment of the present. You know about something that is true today, some currently observable fact that causes you to have this worry about the future. But that "something" is left unspoken. It is trapped inside you.

> Now, suppose I say to you instead, "I just noticed the tread on my car tires has worn all the way down, so I'm worried that I'll get into a car accident on my way home from work."
>
> Now, your first response might be, "Get new tires! Let's call my garage. They can send out a truck that will replace your car tires right here in the parking lot."

Distinguishing this **cause**, defined as "an existing condition, a fact," from the **effect** initiates a much more useful conversation about that risk. With just a few extra words, you and your teammates can understand *why* you have a particular worry, and this often points directly, as the above example shows, to *how* you might mitigate it.

So instead of saying, "The design won't work," you might say something like, "We have not held a design review yet, so I'm concerned the design won't work." It is surprising how often simply stating a **cause** changes how the team listens from "hearing a complaint" to "raising an issue worth responding to."

What happens when you start describing a risk by stating its **cause**?

Because the **cause** is something that is currently so, it grounds the conversation in facts rather than opinions. There should be general agreement that the cause is true, but it is important to confirm that. Perhaps the design review, in fact, did take place, but you were not aware of it. By clearing that up, the "worry" that was keeping you awake at night is efficiently cleaned away. In our experience, rapidly dispelling concerns team members thought were risks, but were really just breakdowns in information sharing, is incredibly useful. The ability to take these concerns off the table frees the team to focus on risks that matter and not fritter away their energy (as often happens) on issues that are not issues.

After establishing **cause** and **effect**, it is critical to clarify how it matters on your project. This leads to questions such as, "If that future bad outcome were to occur, what **impact** would it have?" and "Why should the project management and shareholders care about this risk?" Here are some examples of typical impacts: that the failure to implement a feature will lead to the loss of a target customer, that a delivery date will slip, or that a cost will increase. It may turn out mitigating the impact is the right way to spend resources. The team has many more mitigation options at the front end of the project than they will later—generally at a lower cost.

One of the consequences of having a team *get in the habit* of structuring all its risk conversations, so it explicitly distinguishes **causes**, **effects**, and **impacts**, is the "drama" around risk conversations goes down. The complaining, the not listening, the worries that go nowhere—all those things simply are less interesting and happen less often.

As one of our clients once told us, "We just spend less time complaining at the water cooler."

CEI FORM: DESCRIBING RISKS TO CAUSE ACTION

The language game we are proposing has this structure, which we often refer to as the CEI form for describing risks:

- ◆ **Cause:** An existing, observable condition, a fact
- ◆ **Effect:** The possible future bad outcome
- ◆ **Impact:** What would matter if that outcome happened— why management would care

Let's look at an example of how this conversation plays out in practice:

Harley: The database will never work.

Benoit: Yeah, that's a bummer. There's no way the project will be successful.

What if Benoit responded differently, to flip Harley's complaint into a channel for action?

Harley: The database will never work.

Benoit: Is there something you're noticing, right now, that is making you worried about that?

Harley: Yeah, we need to move on to this new database back end because our current one won't give us the performance we need. But we have no experience with it, and I'm positive we're going to build out the entire database and only then discover there's some limitation we didn't think about that's going to screw everything up.

Benoit: What's the worst that could happen?

Harley: What's the worst that could happen? We'll have to redesign the entire database system, and the whole thing will take twice as long!

Benoit: What do you think we might do about it?

Harley: I probably should, at the very least, read through the new database system manual. Who knows, we might be fine! Maybe my contact at the vendor could find someone who knows their system and at least review our design plan. There are a few specific tests I can think of off the top of my head, but they'd take some time to run. While I'm doing that, can we get Layla to see if we can deliver two weeks later? That way, if we do have to redesign, we'll have time.

Benoit: Think about it and give the vendor a call. Let's meet this afternoon and see what it would look like to add those to the schedule. I'd rather take a couple of days now, so we don't have to throw away the database subsystem and rebuild it. Make sure you submit your risk to Katja, so it gets on the *risk action plan*.

Harley pulls up the risk spreadsheet and submits this new risk:

- Cause: We have no previous experience with the selected database back-end system.

- Effect: We may have to rebuild the database using the old back end.

- Impact: The schedule would be delayed two weeks, and we would miss the date we promised our target customer.

Our teams are amazed by how much information can be clearly and quickly communicated by using this format.

Do you see what Benoit did? He took Harley's initial concern ("worry") and broke it down into three parts. In RUF, we label those parts **cause**, **effect**, and **impact**. Whenever someone voices a complaint or concern regarding your project, get into the habit of asking the question, "What is the cause/effect/impact that expresses what you are worried about?" Let's take a deeper look at this language.

Cause: An Existing Condition, a Fact

The **cause** of a risk is something that is currently true in the environment of your project. Because of that cause, you have some worry or concern. In the dialogue above, Harley is concerned the database might not work, but the thing that is true today is that a decision was made to build on top of a new, unfamiliar database back end. Language describing *that decision* is the **cause**.

Effect: A Possible Future Bad Outcome

A risk's **effect** is the problem that might materialize at some point later in the project. It is the "lightning" that will strike your project late in the game when it is expensive to fix.

Note: If a problem is already present, you haven't identified a **risk**; you've identified an **issue**. It's not a *possibility* that something will go wrong; something *has* gone wrong. As you are discussing risks, don't fool yourself into being committed to the success of a project in the face of something that might happen when it has already happened. Deal with it. We say, "When the house is already on fire, you no longer have a fire risk."

Impact: Why the Team and Management Should Care

The **impact** of a risk describes what the consequences will be, if the effect were to happen, if the lightning were to strike. In the above example, Harley was rapidly able to assess the impact of his risk: the time required to deliver the database system will double.

Think of the **impact** in terms of how management would view it. If it were to delay the project, how long might it be delayed? If it were to cause a feature to fall out, what's the loss in value of losing that feature? Why would management care?

It's not uncommon, after distinguishing the **impact** of a risk,

that you realize your risk isn't as bad as you thought it was—
even if it happened, the project would still succeed. Or you
might discover it's far worse.

GETTING INTO ACTION

Addressing the risks of your project starts at the beginning.
Management of your risks involves three types of activities:

♦ **Identification:** Leverage the wisdom of your cross-functional team to access the whole range of reasons your
project might fail. The goal is to get these risks out of
your blind spot and onto a **risk action plan**, where the
team can address them.

♦ **Prioritization:** RUF prioritizes risks from super high to
low. Getting the prioritization correct is critical, because
this is what guides your allocation of scarce mitigation resources.

♦ **Mitigation:** The whole point of talking about risks is to
cause action. This requires scheduling activities and assigning resources—people, time, and money. Your team needs
to be in urgent action on its super-high and high risks.

You want risk identification to be as easy and frictionless as
possible for the entire span of your project. You want members of your team to submit risks to your **risk action plan** even
when they *suspect* there is something to worry about. When
in doubt, get them on the risk action plan—you'll sort them
out later when you prioritize. When we notice teams submitting risks about the "quality of food in meetings" as a reason

their project might fail, then we know the bar for submitting risks is sufficiently low!

Your team culture should reflect two things: that identifying risks is required of all team members, and when team members identify risks, they are the bearers of "good news," not "bad news."

However, as a consequence, you will have a large number of risks to manage. Healthy **risk action plans** have dozens of risks on them. Therefore, careful prioritization is imperative, and it is why incoming risk reports must be assigned an owner and a prioritization quickly and with rigor. We will describe in detail the prioritization strategy when we talk about the **risk action plan** in part 2. For the moment, note that your team will focus and track obsessively their super-high and high risks. During the **commitment phase** of your project, you will be adjusting all aspects of the project definition, including its scope, who is on the team, and how much time you require, to either push those risks outside of the project or assure the team can mitigate them.

Based on the assignment of an owner, prioritization, and initial assessment, it may be the risk arises because of a simple misunderstanding (e.g., one subteam thought there was a terrible risk, not knowing that another subteam had completely handled it). These will get prioritized as "low" (if they still need to be tracked) or "mitigated" (if they are no longer a risk).

The goal of mitigation is to reduce the risk to a level that allows the team to commit (or remain committed) to their project, that it will be delivered as defined, on time. For any given risk, you should not think of doing "as much mitigation as possible." Instead, determine the "mitigation necessary to achieve (or retain) the commitment of the team to the successful completion of the project."

Risk identification and mitigation does not happen by accident, nor does it come for free. Project leaders must assure that both time and resources are allocated for these activities. The **weekly accountability meetings** are an example of such an allocation. For larger projects, the project leader will gather the other **track leaders** (described in part 2) on a regular basis, specifically to review the **risk action plan**, to make sure that resources are being properly allocated, and that mitigation is happening for top risks.

Proposing Mitigations

The focus is on action, so we train teams to get creative about how they might mitigate a risk from the moment the risk is first identified. In our example above, Harley was easily able to suggest several different approaches to mitigating the risk that he himself identified. This is quite common. We push anyone on a team who identifies a risk to come up with several potential mitigating actions *at the time she submits it.* Our rule of thumb: at least five.

A proposed mitigation might resolve a risk, or it might partially resolve a risk, or it might make team members smarter about steps they should take next to resolve the risk. It might address the cause as a suggestion that the current circumstance be changed. It might reduce the effect of the risk—for example, by funding a backup plan. Finally, it could address the impact—for example, by changing who is the target customer, and making the corresponding tradeoffs.

You can see these various techniques in Harley's proposed mitigations:

- Because the cause is lack of experience with the database system, his proposal to read through the system manual increases his level of familiarity with the system. This mitigation attacks the cause.

- To reduce the likelihood of having to redesign the database, he proposes engaging the vendor to review their design. This mitigation attacks the effect.

- When he proposes they renegotiate the delivery date with their customer, he is allowing for the possibility they will have to redo the design, but the customer won't notice. This mitigation attacks the impact.

Note there is no **commitment** to do any of these things— they are proposals. As the team decides what they need to do to commit to their project definition in the face of this risk, those decisions will be reflected in real work in the form of **action items** with accountable owners and due dates that will be added to the **weekly schedule**.

Prioritizing Risk

We want teams to set a low bar for the *identification* of risks. In RUF, this means submitting a risk to the **risk action plan**. Don't discourage your team from submitting "dumb" risks; they may well contain the seeds of something important. Err on the side of **transparency**.

We often notice teams trying to optimize their behavior around risk mitigation by thinking about "how serious" the risk impacts are and how likely the risks are to happen. They may deploy complex probabilistic methodologies—your team may use Failure Mode and Effects Analysis (FMEA), Fault Tree Analysis (FTA), or Capability Maturity Modeling (CMM) to make these determinations.

> **Risk action plan:** The RUF structure that drives the team to capture risks and tracks actions to mitigate them throughout the project. A spreadsheet (or other tool such as Atlassian Jira with appropriate templates) containing a list of risks in CEI form, with priorities, owners, and proposed mitigations.
>
> **RAP sheet:** What the cool kids call the **risk action plan**.
>
> **A RAP:** An entry representing one risk on the **RAP sheet**. As in, "Please submit that risk as a RAP."

These approaches often get in the way of the early identification and mitigation of risks. They create a "chicken and egg" problem, where the team feels they cannot mitigate risks until they model their risks, and they cannot model their risks until they have defined their project or completed its designs.

Teams, in our experience, are strongly biased to be too optimistic and to procrastinate. They underestimate the impact of problems they don't know how to solve. So while certain projects may require and benefit from sophisticated modeling, we don't want that to stand in the way of getting into action on risks early.

These classic strategies for prioritizing risks involve weighting their impact by the likelihood they'll happen. However, when the team has little experience in the risk, they are really in no position to accurately assess its likelihood. The resulting prioritization will be misleading.

To solve this conundrum, we focus teams on a simple question: "Have we (or anyone) successfully mitigated this risk before?" If the answer is no, consider the risk to be high. This helps teams avoid the common pitfall of focusing too much attention on the risks they understand well and not enough time on the risks that are unfamiliar or difficult to assess or articulate.

FOCUSING TEAMS ON RISK

Benoit asked Harley to submit his risk to the **risk action plan**. We train teams to respond to every suggestion of a risk with, "Have you submitted it to the **risk action plan** yet?" (The cool kids call the **risk action plan** the **RAP sheet**, and they'd say, "Did you submit a **RAP**?")

The **risk action plan** is the RUF structure that drives risk identification and mitigation on the project. By breaking down risks into **CEI form**, you ensure they move your team out of the world of complaints and into the world of action. From the beginning of the project, the team is holding **weekly**

accountability meetings and surfacing the top risks on the project. If a team member notices the project has a risk that isn't on the **risk action plan**, she must submit it.

Every submitted risk is assigned an owner who is accountable for getting the risk mitigated to the extent the project requires. In our example, Benoit is both the person who raises the risk (because he is submitting it to the **risk action plan**, he is the "submitter") and the person who knows the most about what it would take to mitigate the risk. He is the obvious candidate to own the risk.

The language, metrics, structures, and practices of RUF are all tightly interrelated. Taken together, they focus on changing the culture of your team to identify and mitigate risks early. Once you have a firm grasp of the ideas and philosophy described in part 1, part 2 will show you how to deploy these ideas on your project using the RUF practices and tools.

THINGS TO REMEMBER

◆ Having a culture in which risk conversations are frequent and celebrated is extraordinary and powerful. Teams and their management must make risk conversations a required contribution of every team member.

◆ Ritualizing the use of Risk Up Front's language of **cause**, **effect**, and **impact** within your team transforms their ability to identify and mitigate risks.

◆ Make it easy to surface risks, even trivial ones. Don't allow your team members to self-censor.

◆ Being specific in the **cause** of a risk reduces drama and increases the likelihood of action.

◆ Prioritize your risks based on familiarity, not severity. The risks you have the least experience with are the most dangerous.

◆ Get creative when exploring mitigations. Outlandish suggestions often create paths to ideal solutions.

PART 2

STRUCTURES, TOOLS, PRACTICES

A cautionary tale, followed by some questions:

> Jackie, your manager, tells you she needs a revision of your product for a key customer, who needs some core features redesigned to increase performance by 50 percent. She says they need it by the end of the quarter, six weeks away. "I'm counting on you," she says.
>
> You tell her you'll do your best.
>
> After checking with some of your colleagues, you sketch out a brief spec describing what's needed and a list of things to design, build, and test, and you enter them into a Microsoft Project schedule.
>
> You ask around to see who has time and write down a list of names of people you can recruit. It seems everyone from Quality Assurance is busy for the next month on another project, but that's OK because you won't be able to test anything before then anyway.
>
> With the people whom you think you can get to work on your project, Microsoft Project estimates it will take longer than a quarter to get done, by three or four weeks.
>
> So you move some tasks around, cut some functions out, shorten the testing time, and you think you can pull it in under the wire, if all goes well.
>
> You invite everyone on your list to a meeting on Friday, but too many people are out of the office, so you reinvite them for the following Monday. That works better.
>
> At the meeting, you repeat Jackie's request, walk them through the schedule, and ask if it will work, or if anything stands in the way.
>
> Some people mention a few concerns: "I think Pramila is going to be on vacation next week, but I'm not sure." Pramila, your best engineer, was on your list, but she couldn't come to this meeting.

You turn to Ichiko.

"I'll go talk to Pramila, but Ichiko," you ask, "do you think you can build Pramila's piece if necessary?"

"I think so," Ichiko says.

You write that issue down, along with the other concerns that were raised. You add your own concern that there isn't enough time allocated for testing.

"OK, that seems to be it. Are we all on board?" you say.

"Yes, we'll do our best!" they say.

You tell Jackie you've reviewed the schedule with the team, and they've already started. "Great work. Thank you!" Jackie says.

Some questions to ask yourself:

1. Have you ever been on a project like this? How did it go?
2. Predict the future. What would you say will likely happen by the end of the quarter?
3. What, specifically, might you do differently to achieve a different result?

Even though this example describes only the period from when Jackie describes the opportunity through the end of the first team meeting, a number of things happened, roles were assigned, lists were made, and risks (or at least "concerns") were recorded. You put in place a "structure" and launched a "project." Then what happened?

Of course, you know how this story continues.

It turns out the other project Quality Assurance was busy with was delayed, so when the time arrived at which you were scheduled to begin testing, you find yourself going to Jackie, saying, "I'm sorry, but we're not going to be done by the end of the quarter. If QA finishes their project next week, we'll be able to do a quick testing cycle. You'll need to tell the customer they won't get their revision next week; it will be ready in two weeks."

Jackie says, "That's very unfortunate. I'll see if we can save the account. What went wrong?" You pull out your list of concerns from the first meeting and say, "Well, we were afraid that we were cutting QA close, and it turns out we were." "Well, that makes sense," Jackie replied.

When the QA team finally was free to assess your changes, their lead test engineer reviewed it and got back to you. "We're going to have to create a new test harness if you want us to check your performance specs. That'll take a week. Then we can finish the tests in another week." "But I allotted only one," you say. "Can you pull it in?" Your tester suggests, "Well, we could skip the performance tests altogether..."

Risk Up Front changes what happens at the front edge of your project so you get better results at the end of your project. But this is important: Those lists we described in the example—the schedule, the team list, the risk list? In RUF, you still have them. But "having the right list" (or any list) or "having the right spec" (or any spec) is not the fundamentally important thing. You can see what's missing:

♦ **Transparency:** We thought the right people understood what the project required, but we did not insist on clarifying with the QA team what we needed and what they needed from the start.

- **Accountability:** Who is on the hook to build Pramila's module if she can't?

- **Integrity:** We told Jackie we'd be done by the end of the quarter, but we already had a list of unresolved reasons why we might not be able to.

- **Commitment:** We accepted, in fact we celebrated, the team's "I'll do my best!" while perfectly aware that this would not be sufficient to deliver a successful project.

We see in this example specific failures of **accountability, transparency, integrity**, and **commitment**. Here's another question to think about. Who is accountable on this project for ensuring these failures are actually rectified? Who cares that these elements are missing? You? Jackie? Pramila? Ichiko? The engineer from QA who wasn't in the room?

The fact is, if you don't have the organizational structures and practices that establish these issues front and center before the team on day one, it doesn't matter, because these issues will land squarely in their blind spot. That is why structure is so important and why Risk Up Front is so opinionated that certain structures and practices must be established on your project from the very beginning. Then as the project unfolds, these structures and practices must be maintained with the utmost rigor, because breakdowns of **accountability, transparency, integrity**, and **commitment** that may jeopardize your project can occur in any part of your project at any time.

Part 2 is where the rubber hits the road. We'll go through the tools and steps of applying RUF techniques to your project and your team. We just want to reiterate the importance of rigor. If you find your team reviewing paperwork and not actively searching for and improving its **transparency** and **integrity**, you won't have a successful project; you'll simply have a pile of paper. If your team is committing to get things done, and things are not getting done, you simply have a pile of promises. As one of our clients told us, "Excellent paperwork is the booby prize."

CHAPTER 6

THE RISK UP FRONT PROJECT TIMELINE

We'll start by discussing how projects unfold over time and by describing the important decision points to make explicit. We'll also look at the key structural elements you'll put in place. Because team meetings are an important element of several RUF practices (and because we've seen so many bad meetings), we will conclude this chapter with our techniques for running an effective meeting that brings the principles of RUF to life.

DECISION POINTS

One of the most basic aspects of organizing any project is being able to account for its cost and value. This is most often monetary cost (wages, materials, rents), but even if your team consists of volunteers, you must make choices about how you deploy them to get the results you all want.

One obvious problem with the common "fuzzy front end" to projects is people find themselves working on getting the project done before anyone has made any decision that the project is worth doing. People begin to think of that work as "the project" while the project is "an idea possibly worth pursuing" rather than "We've made a decision to spend money to do it." That work spins wider and deeper, other projects get shortchanged or pushed aside, and the ability to set priorities goes out the window. The first step to getting this process under control is to be clear whether a project has started or not. Even while your team has its list of projects you are considering—future projects, possible projects—you will want to label explicitly which are your active projects so there is no confusion.

Here is how that looks. When you talk about your projects, people will assume you are talking about active projects, but it is important to be clear about which of four states your projects are in:

♦ **Proposed:** Projects that you might do, are thinking of doing, are vaguely looming on some future product road map, and so on.

♦ **Budgeted:** A decision has been made for these projects to begin definition within the current budgeting period, but they haven't started yet. The budget reflects some rough estimate of what these projects will require.

♦ **Active:** Projects that have officially started and are consuming resources.

♦ **Closed:** Projects that have been completed or abandoned.

Do not expend the project team's time and effort on projects that aren't active. Do not live in a world where you have projects that are sort of active. Do not let there be confusion about whether a project is active or not. If a project is blocked from making progress, use your resources to get it unblocked (if it is worth doing), or abandon it, and perhaps, if appropriate, propose to initiate it later. We see projects fail when teams lose momentum and urgency, especially around identifying and mitigating risks, because the project is stuck, and so the team drifts away to do other stuff. Your team might think of this as "making the best use of our time," but it represents the common failure of focusing on what you know, instead of focusing on identifying and mitigating risks in your blind spot.

If you are a manager who makes decisions on project budgets, there are three key decision points you are accountable for. **Transparency** requires everyone in your organization to be clear on what you decide. When we begin working with organizations, both management and team members are often too comfortable having these decisions be implicit or unspoken. No longer.

Decision #1: The Decision to Begin

If you want your team to work on a project, you need to be crystal clear that you are deciding to start that project. But by making that decision, what have you committed to?

Remember the value of starting from zero.

When you have trained your team to assume projects begin without knowing what the project is, you will realize the first decision is to deploy a team to define and commit to the

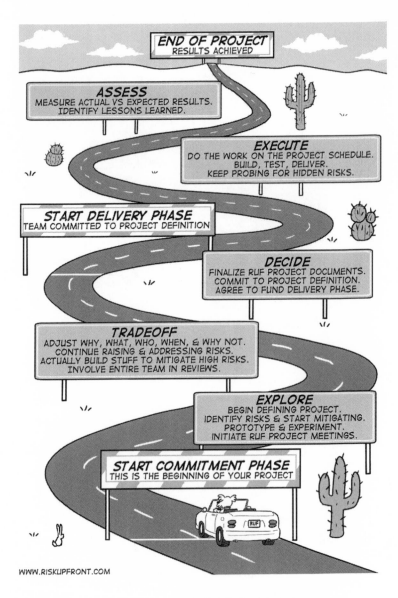

Fig. 19: The path of a Risk Up Front project.

right **5W tradeoff** for this project. The team will front-load the project with the focus, resources, and urgency necessary to wrestle the project into a shape they and their management can agree is worth executing.

If you are a manager, your decision to begin a project in this way does not mean you are extracting any promise or **commitment** from the team to deliver any particular result by any particular deadline. Except for the most trivial projects, you don't want to go to your team and say, "Deliver result X by date Y," because it forecloses their opportunity to define a result they can commit to deliver. You need to explicitly send them off with the mission to figure out what is the fully defined project that is both valuable and achievable. They need the time to identify what that is and then determine if they can commit to achieve it. Too many project teams operate, unsuccessfully, under the narrative, "Management gave us no choice..."

You are instead asking a team (or, more specifically, their **project leader**), to whom you present a "compelling opportunity" or a "good idea," to initiate the process of figuring out if and how that opportunity can best be exploited.

By insisting that the only useful **project definition** is one having the robust **commitment** of the team, you are commissioning them to invest time and resources to identify and mitigate risks early.

This decision initiates the RUF **commitment phase**. During this phase, the team, with your review and input along the way, will come back to you with one of two outcomes: either a **commitment** to achieve some result by a date (though it may look different from what you originally proposed), or the discovery that the opportunity turns out not to be worth pursuing—there was no achievable tradeoff that made economic sense. In the latter case, you will terminate the project with minimal wasted effort. This often happens when the team and management discover "the time is not ripe" to pursue an opportunity—of course, the project can be restarted with a new **commitment phase** later, when the time is ripe.

When you make the decision to begin the **commitment phase** of a project, you must ensure certain elements are in place. Without these, the commitment phase hasn't actually started:

1. You have designated an empowered and accountable **project leader**.

2. You have identified the **tracks** of the project, and designated a **track leader** for each track.

3. You have developed a first draft (no matter how skeletal) of the **project statement**.

Decision #2: The Decision to Deliver

In the interesting case, the team will come back to you with a **commitment** to achieve a result represented by their clear identification of a **5W tradeoff**: to achieve a measurable result for an identified customer, using committed resources, by a clear deadline, in the face of identified risks.

As a manager, you need to ensure three things: the tradeoff is clear and measurable, the result is valuable, and the team is committed. If those three things are true, then you can make the decision to execute the project, and the team will do what they've determined is necessary to achieve the given result.

During the **delivery phase**, the team will continue to track its performance, identify and mitigate risks, and manage breakdowns that might occur.

If you are working on a complex project with an established project management method that involves multiple phases, this works fine with RUF. The RUF boundary between the **commitment phase** and the **delivery phase** may correspond naturally to one of the phase gates in your methodology, though it need not. We merely require there be a point in time where everyone is clear that (1) the team has established their **commitment** to deliver a result, and (2) management has established they are willing to pay for the delivery of the result that the team committed to, with the shared understanding that it will be so, even in the face of circumstances.

The decision to begin the **delivery phase** is the decision that ends the **commitment phase**. This means that three things must be true:

1. The **core** and **extended team** have committed to deliver the project as defined by the **project statement**. Have appropriate project team members *sign* the project statement.

2. **Risks** have been identified and mitigated to the level that makes the team commitment credible.

3. Cross-functional senior management has reviewed the project statement, risks, and other appropriate project information. Preferably, this review takes place in a meeting with those senior managers face to face with each other and with the core team. After that, the accountable executive explicitly makes and communicates the decision to begin the **delivery phase**.

Decision #3: The Decision to End

> **Done:** The results we committed to achieve are inarguably achieved.
>
> **Not done:** Committed results have not (yet) been achieved. Results other than what were committed were achieved. Sort of done, partly done, almost done, done enough—these are all in the category of "not done."

When the team has demonstrated that the agreed-upon results are achieved, the project is declared **done** and is ended. The resources allocated to that project are released and can be used on other projects. Conversely, if team members are still required to work on the project, the project is, by definition, **not done**.

Sometimes projects need to be ended before achieving their committed objective when they fail to achieve an interim milestone or if the market or organizational priorities have shifted. Don't let a decision to prematurely terminate a project pass quietly. For projects that are abandoned, make clear to the team why the decision was made. If there is a forward-looking plan to pursue that opportunity, make that clear too.

For projects that are successfully concluded, *do not skip the celebration*. Teams need this ritual, acknowledging the effort they have expended and the value they have created.

THE PROJECT LEADER

Every active project must have a single, empowered, accountable **project leader**. The project leader ensures that everything the project needs to happen, happens. This is a *causal* accountability. It *does not* entail the project leader will necessarily be the person who does the actual work or *make* the actual decision. Their job is to make sure each required decision is made by the right person.

More specifically, the project leader must:

♦ Resolve all issues and obstacles that are blocking the team's progress.

♦ Assemble and lead a cross-functional project team to define and achieve a committed **project definition**.

♦ Lead the team to act with rigorous **accountability, transparency, integrity**, and **commitment** on the project, day to day. Notice and respond to situations where these principles are compromised.

♦ Own the **weekly accountability meeting (WAM)** while the project is active.

♦ Cause the **integrity** of the team, week by week, and transparently report its status to the team and to management.

♦ Ensure the **integrity** of the RUF **project documents**, and transparently communicate them throughout the team and management.

♦ During the **commitment phase**, lead the team through a rigorous process to discover the **5W tradeoff** for the project, causing the team to identify and mitigate risks, and ultimately secure the team's robust **commitment** to achieve the project results.

♦ Own and run the **definition meetings**.

♦ During the **delivery phase**, continue running **WAMs** and tracking the **integrity** of the team's commitments. Lead the team to address breakdowns if and when they occur.

♦ Host the team celebration when success is achieved.

In RUF, project leadership is a *role*; it is not a "job title." In some organizations the **project leader** naturally comes from a specific functional group, for example, a project management group or the program office. But that role, or "hat," can be worn by a team member from *any* functional group. Depending on the nature or size of the project, we often see project leaders from engineering, product management, finance or other functions. RUF only requires that *every* project have a designated project leader from the start. Remember, the project leader role is distinct from the other accountabilities that this team member may also have on the project, for example, they also may be a track lead or subject matter expert. It is important to recognize that fulfilling the role of project leader will require time and energy that take away from that team member's capacity to perform other roles.

A word on singular leadership: We have seen organizational structures that assign co-leaders or co-managers for projects. This is a bad idea for at least two reasons. First, when multiple people are accountable for a result, none are accountable.

Designating multiple owners simply raises the risk that each will expect the other to track and manage the delivery of some result. The need to intervene when a breakdown occurs has reduced urgency, because both understand there's someone else on the hook to handle it.

Second, it is unclear to whom a team member should raise an issue, thinking, "Which one of the accountable owners should I bother?" This creates a completely unnecessary friction that causes issues and risks to be swept under the rug. In principle, you might suggest, this shouldn't happen. In practice, it happens all the time. If you think you need co-leaders, instead either (1) explicitly divide their accountabilities so they do not overlap—this restores singular accountability—and/or (2) let one be, explicitly, the backup or delegate of the other.

In RUF, all **accountability** is understood to be *causal*. When you agree to be held accountable, you are saying you will cause something to be done. Thus, a **project leader** can delegate any of the work, while remaining on the hook to make sure the required results are achieved.

THE CROSS-FUNCTIONAL PROJECT TEAM

Let's talk about what we mean when we say a project team must be "cross-functional." On engineering or manufacturing projects, we often see the only people in the room are engineers. They don't communicate as a group with people in other areas—marketing, sales, legal, compliance, operations. They relate to those areas as services, saying things like, "We need work from those people, but they are not *on the team.*" Sometimes we are introduced to organizations where we notice these groups don't even get along. They don't speak the same language, and they are interested in different things.

Teams must fight against the organization's tendency to isolate activity in this way. This dynamic of "silo thinking" is alive and well in many organizations. We see this where individuals are focused on their functional group, and work product is passed from one silo to the next with minimal cross-functional transparency and review.

Allowing these functions to stay inside their silos and only communicate through, for example, the **project leader**, or only when the engineers decide a question needs to be answered, creates a variety of risks. There are risks that decisions being made in one area affect another area in ways that will only be discovered late in the project. For example, we see this when engineering decides to build something operations says they can't support. Or when marketing identifies a product feature that runs headlong into a legal or regulatory constraint. Another common problem arises when a team consists of only engineers, who are trained to solve whatever problems you put in front of them—they will feel an inexorable pull to solve their marketing, legal, support, and testing problems themselves, as best they can. To those engineers, attempting to solve the problem themselves seems easier than getting an expert from one of those departments to show up to a **definition meeting**.

Organizing Project Teams

Teams and their management need to be crystal clear as to who is on the team and who is not. It is surprising how often our clients cannot answer the simple question, "Who is on the team?" (Or, for an individual, "Am I on the team?"). Projects fail for lack of clarity about who is accountable for delivering what the project requires. You therefore want to be transparent about who is on the team, which is why the integrity of the RUF **team list** is so important.

The **project team** consists of exactly the set of individuals who are accountable for delivering the things that the project requires for the project to be successful.

If you own any deliverable, any action item, or any risk on which the project's success depends, you are on the project team.

Does that mean you are in every meeting? Probably not. Are you in every weekly accountability meeting or definition meeting? For smaller projects (fewer than around twelve project team members), the answer is yes. For larger projects, RUF introduces some structures for organizing teams.

For substantial projects, think of your team along these four lines:

Project team: These are the individuals who have accountabilities and deliverables on the project. Some members will have many accountabilities, some will have few—they are all on the team. For example, your lead engineer may have

Fig. 20: The organization of project teams.

responsibilities in many areas of your project; it may be their full-time job. In contrast, your team member from the legal department may have only a few accountabilities, such as approving vendor contracts. They spend only a fraction of their time on your project. But both are listed on the project team list.

Core team: People on the core team form a subset of the **project team**. They are required at all **weekly accountability meetings** and **definition meetings**. Think of the core team as the set of team members that can speak to "90 percent of the deliverables and 90 percent of the risks and issues" on the project. They are active on the project from the beginning. The core team must always be cross-functional and have the critical members necessary to bring the project to a profitable completion. If your core team consists of only engineers, it is not cross-functional.

Extended team: These are members of the **project team** who are not part of the **core team**. They typically have few account-abilities or limited participation. Identify people you need on your extended team up front and secure their participation. They need to ensure they will be ready and available when you eventually need them. For example, a senior engineer may be needed to attend only a critical design review scheduled halfway through the project. A **functional manager** may have no accountability to your project other than to make sure that a team member in their function is properly supported. Even extended team members must know what the project is counting on them to deliver, and they must commit, like the rest of the team. Plan to give even extended team members a project T-shirt.

You must pull the **extended team** into your definition process at least once during the commitment phase so you have their perspective on risks. Do not do this later than the "next to last" definition meeting so that the team has time to address these risks.

Tracks: How the project activities are grouped into project tracks depends on your organization and on your project— they may correspond to departments or groups, such as product marketing, engineering, legal, and so on. The key is to make sure each of the tracks on your project is covered by an accountable **owner**, identified as the **track leader**. Each activity on the project is associated with a particular track—track leaders manage those streams of activity. Many of our clients find that it is useful to standardize a default set of tracks that represent the minimum level of cross-functionality necessary to complete the sort of projects they typically undertake. Project leadership may modify the types and number of tracks as long as that is done transparently.

Every project has a "project management" track; its track leader is the project leader herself. The project management track also may contain activities that don't have any other obvious home, such as Finance and HR.

These **track leaders** form the leadership team of the project. They must cooperate as colleagues who will support one another to ensure the entire project is working and will be successful. The project leader manages the other track leaders to ensure progress and success on the project. This limits the number of track leaders a project can have—we find that eight is the practical maximum. Track leaders, of course, are on the **core team**.

"Track leadership" is a hat any **core team** member can wear on a project. A track leader need not be the most senior member of that function, and they may not have the word *manager* in their job title. They simply must have the ability and time to manage the people and activities of their track.

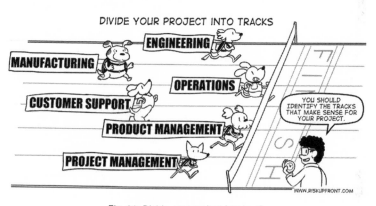

Fig. 21: Divide your project into tracks.

As the **project leader**, when you are designing the team for your RUF project, we expect you to engage every person who will be accountable for some deliverable, without which the project might fail. If at some point you expect to involve quality assurance or testing, then someone accountable for testing will be on the **cross-functional project team**. If your project deliverable must pass a regulatory, legal, or compliance sign-off, then whoever is accountable for making sure that sign-off succeeds must be on your project team. If your deliverable is a product you expect to sell for a profit, then someone accountable for making sure it is salable and properly priced (say, from sales or product marketing) must be on the project team.

This is not to say every member of the project team is busy on the project, 100 percent, at all times. It means at some point, you are going to count on them. The team is going to count on them. Remember, by the end of the **commitment phase**, each team member commits not to getting her own piece done but rather to the success of the project. Without that level of trust, **commitment** becomes impossible: how can I commit to a result that depends on a contributor if I don't know who they are (or if they even exist) or don't trust their commitment to deliver?

When you as a **project leader** start a project, you will write down your best guess as to who should be on the **core team**. You may have to negotiate with other teams, identify alternatives, horse-trade resources, whatever. Remember, our rule of thumb is the **core team** should be able to speak capably to about 90 percent of the deliverables and risks the project will entail. Even without knowing exactly what the project will ultimately require, we find this provides a useful guide.

When you first assemble your **core team**, all you will know is it is the wrong team. You just don't know *in what way* it is wrong. This is one of the first questions your empowered and accountable **core team** will explore as they identify and adjust who should be in the core and extended groups. The team itself will make the corrections necessary to evolve itself into the right team for the project. Changes to team membership, just like any other project changes, are less expensive when made early. Your aim is that team membership should be stable during the **delivery phase**.

When the **core team** comes together for the first **definition meeting** and starts to surface risks and make tradeoffs, they may identify additional individuals who will need to be involved. Over the course of the **commitment phase**, as the team adjusts what is in and out of scope, and as the team uncovers issues that it was blind to, the composition of the **project team** can be expected to change.

We emphasize this because it is one of the fundamental premises underlying Risk Up Front: you have no greater tool than the empowered and accountable **cross-functional project team** for making corrections to your project. You must leverage this from the start of your project, and you will continue to rely on it throughout the course of your project.

Substantial, complex projects require a core team, tracks, and track leaders. On smaller projects, the core team may be the same as the entire project team. At a small startup, your core team may be _the entire company_.

STRUCTURES FOR COMMUNICATION: SHARING INFORMATION

Although we encounter a wide variety of systems that teams use to plan and communicate internally, RUF focuses on four critical structures: there must be a way for anyone on the project team, and management, to read key project documents that describe the state of the project and the commitments that have been made and the progress toward achieving those commitments.

If your project team has a room set aside where the project team meets and works, these documents can be printed and posted on the wall. The RUF **project documents**, especially the **project statement**, are concise enough to be posted as "wall ware"—that is infinitely more useful than "drawer ware."

Moreover, especially if your team members are not all in one geographic location, you'll need an online, shared computer repository for your project documents.

There are many tools that support this—a shared folder on Google Drive can work, the Atlassian document management toolset is used by many of our clients, even Microsoft Share-Point can work. RUF **project documents** must be readable by the team and management and writable by the **project leader** or her delegates. On large projects, there may be a project librarian or documents team. Other subgroups on the project may have their own folders (readable team-wide, writable by the document owner) for their own project documents, drafts, specs, spreadsheets, tool data sets, and so forth.

We haven't talked about the many forms of "chat" (IRC, Slack, Asana, Symphony, Google Hangout, and so on) that teams, especially geographically distributed teams, use. Some teams use these tools casually; some impose structure and workflow in their use of these tools. But we want to be clear that communication via project documents is held to a high standard with respect to **transparency** and **integrity**. The words on those documents are carefully chosen. Chat forums are much more narrowly focused on workflow and issue resolution and are not a "record" for project decisions. You may use these tools to discuss issues and then move clear decisions to formal documents.

These communications tools cannot replace face-to-face meetings for solving certain kinds of problems, especially exploratory and **DKDK** conversations.

EXCELLENT MEETINGS

In our experience, project teams complain (often loudly) about having too many meetings. At the same time, paradoxically, they tell us they suffer from having too few meetings ("It's so hard to get everyone in one room!"). We frequently hear teams complain meeting time is wasted.

Running a good meeting takes skill and experience. If you don't like how your meetings are working for you, explicitly focus on developing your organization's competency in running excellent meetings. You and your team deserve it.

That said, we are going to describe to you how we approach meetings, especially those that are critical to Risk Up Front. We'll start with basic meeting best practices.

When to Call a Meeting

A meeting is a tool—you use it to get something done. It is good for some things, though not everything. When you need team members to talk face-to-face to solve a problem or make a decision in real time, you need a meeting. Example: If you find your team unable to negotiate a decision, even after rounds and rounds of memos and emails, it often pays to lock them together in a room; they can leave when the decision is made.

The first step to having better meetings starts before the meeting happens: Decide and transparently communicate three things:

◆ What does the meeting need to accomplish to be successful?

◆ Who is the **owner** who requires that result?

◆ Exactly who must participate to achieve that result?

```
From: Jackie
To: Pramila, Irfan, Birgitte
Subject: Decide who owns each track of Tigris
test run for 2.0rc1
Owner: Jackie

Required participants: Pramila, Irfan, Birgitte
Required results: A decision as to who will own
each track of the test run for revision 2.0rc1
action items and risks.

When: 2:00 p.m. Tuesday
```

```
Where: Project Tigris Work Room
We'll discuss what's required and compare
your schedules to make sure the full test suite
gets completed on time. Please review test
plan prior to meeting.
```

There are three types of meetings:

♦ **Issue meetings:** These are meetings used to solve problems and make decisions (prior to the meeting, you don't know the answer to an issue, and *you know* you don't know it). It pays to keep the meeting small and focused on the result, not the process. As experts in your area, you know best when to deploy these meetings. We'll just provide some advice about how to do it better.

♦ **DKDK meetings:** For meetings used to uncover blind spots (prior to the meeting, *you don't know what you don't know*), meeting participation must be broad, and process is critical. These types of meetings, including the **definition meeting** and the **weekly accountability meeting**, are at the core of **Risk Up Front**.

♦ **Informational meetings:** These include the company presentations, "town halls," "live demos" that allow people to learn about things that have happened, decisions that have been made, plans, and so on. These are generally outside the realm of projects, they don't depend on collaboration, and we won't say more about them other than this: don't pretend a meeting is informational if you're depending on it to resolve a problem on a project.

We'll start by reviewing some basic best practices that apply to all your meetings.

There Must Be an Owner

The owner is the person who needs the meeting to solve a specific problem. She has decided it is necessary to get a group of people together in place (or on a call), at the same time, to cause a discussion out of which will come the solution to her problem. For example, the discussion may give the **owner** the information she needs to announce her decision. If the problem gets solved, the meeting was successful.

Identify the Participants

The **owner** decides (and sometimes negotiates prior to the meeting) who will attend her meeting. The trick is to identify the exact group of people who can solve the owner's problem. For that reason, the idea of "optional participants" is counterproductive—don't have them. Either the **owner** believes their participation is required to solve the problem, and on that basis, she needs them to participate, or if their participation is not required, they should not be invited to participate.

If you own the meeting, ask yourself what does each participant get out of the meeting that is valuable to them? Obviously, if you are gathering members of your team to solve a problem that (1) they are needed to help solve the problem, and (2) the project needs that problem to be solved, and (3) the team is committed to the success of the project, then the participants will value getting that problem solved for you. However, if you're calling the entire team to tell you the status of what they're working on, and the other participants don't see why they should care, you're not going to have a good meeting. Competent meeting owners make their meetings worth their participants' time.

Especially for **DKDK** meetings, where it might not be obvious, it is important for the participants to understand why they are needed in the room. If they are not familiar with Risk Up Front and what its practices intend to accomplish, their participation may be weak. They won't contribute effectively to shifting urgent risk identification to the front of the project, which is what you (as the **owner**) need. Remember, your team members are perhaps less familiar—and less comfortable—with these types of meetings, so you will want to explicitly repeat at the beginning of the meeting what the goal is and what level of participation you expect from them.

Establish a culture where you agree to start meetings at their scheduled time, with all the required participants present and ready to go. If one of them is not present, don't start the meeting! Find out, if you are able, whether she is coming late. If so, you can choose explicitly to delay the start of the meeting for when she arrives—you can wait, or you can decide when to reconvene. If it turns out she is unable to attend, abort the scheduled meeting, and reschedule it when the required participants are all available. Teams will often "do their best with the people who showed up," but this is unproductive: if you have the meeting (or pretend to have the meeting) anyway without all the required participants, it means you will end up having that meeting twice—going through it again when the missing participant is in the room.

We want to be clear that starting meetings on time is more than just being considerate of the time of your fellow participants (though of course it is that). When an invitee receives a meeting request, she is being asked for her **commitment** to participate. She is free to say yes or say no. If she says no, the meeting **owner** can find out what's blocking and negotiate alternatives. If she says yes, she is saying that she will be at a meeting at a certain time. If the participants are acting with **integrity** ("We do what we say!"), they will begin the meeting at the appointed time. If they are unable to act with **integrity** in that simple instance, why would we assume they will "do what they say" in other instances? Operating consistently with **integrity** takes practice. Use these simpler opportunities to practice it so it will be second nature when life gets complicated. This is what it looks like to engineer **integrity** into your team's culture.

If you are asked to participate in a meeting, transparently state your **commitment** to attend (on time or ready to go), or if you can't commit to attend, clearly decline. The meeting **owner** can work with a clear "yes" or a clear "no." What is unworkable is when you commit to attend and then don't. That behavior creates a toxic drag on your team's ability to collaboratively solve problems.

Identify the Required Result

Beware of meetings that are billed as "We need to discuss X," "We're going to present Y." Don't focus on what you will do (the task, the activity); focus on what you need to accomplish—the successful result. The **owner** needs to be up front about what outcome the meeting needs to achieve. Here are examples of common meeting results, where the owner needs to do the following:

♦ **Make a decision.** For example, given a problem, the participants are brought together to explore various ways of solving it, their pros and cons, and help the **owner** identify the best one.

♦ **Negotiate agreement.** For example, representatives of different groups need to negotiate an agreement on how their work products will integrate or how they will schedule a handoff.

♦ **Divide up work.** Participants will discuss how to divide up a chunk of work, and the result is the owner will have commitments from the participants to be accountable for activity that will add up to a result she is on the hook to deliver.

♦ **Uncover blind spots** and get the team into action to mitigate risks in a particular area. This happens to be one of the required results of the RUF meetings.

What about an agenda? It turns out, if you are clear on the result you require, you don't need an agenda for most small meetings whose goal is to solve a problem. Get together, focus on getting the result you require, then when you have it, leave. If you focus the team on the required result, you aim the meeting toward getting that result—if you get that result early, you leave early; if you focus the team on a "topic of discussion," you'll fill the allotted meeting time with talk, and you'll never experience the deep joy of adjourning a successful meeting early.

Excellent Meeting Invitations

An excellent meeting starts with an excellent invitation. The invitation should account for the essential components of a meeting to review:

- What is the result the **owner** needs?

- Who are the people who must be present to get that result?

- What do they need to do to prepare so they're ready to get that result?

Note that nowhere in this list do we talk about a meeting agenda—you don't need it in an invitation. For example, suppose Blythe is accountable for the power supply for her project. She needs to get a group together to help her identify which power supply vendor to use for her project. Blythe used to send out meeting requests like this:

```
From: Blythe
Required Attendees: Birgitte, Brad
Optional Attendees: Boris
Subject: Power Supply
Time: June 13, 2016, 10:00—11:00 a.m.

Let's get together to discuss the pros and cons
of our various power supply vendors.
```

But now she knows better. She eliminates optional participants who are not required, focuses the subject line on the required result (in this case, her decision), and tells participants what she needs them to do to prepare and bring to the meeting to make that result possible. In this example, in focusing on getting a decision, Blythe realizes she doesn't need Boris, but she must have Blayne, the contract administrator, because Blayne has to sign off on the actual decision.

```
From: Blythe
Required Attendees: Birgitte, Brad, Blayne
Subject: Decide on Power Supply Vendor
Time: June 13, 2016, 10:00—11:00 a.m.

Please bring to the meeting the results of
your power supply vendor research so we can
finalize this decision.
```

Match Participants to Results

It is wasteful to pack together a group of needed results into a single meeting when the exact set of participants required to solve each problem are not the same. You have people in the room watching others participate in solving problems they don't care about. We expect each member of the meeting to feel her presence is necessary to solve the problem the meeting is addressing. If members don't, then the **owner** didn't pick the participants properly or did not articulate the result they require in a way that is compelling enough to engage the participants. Owners take responsibility for not letting anyone feel her time is wasted in participating in your meetings.

This also means you'll want to schedule one meeting to solve one problem. Then schedule a separate meeting to solve another problem.

DKDK Meetings

One type of meeting central to RUF is not focused on solving a single project-specific problem. Rather, it is a meeting designed to uncover issues and risks in the team's blind spot. We call these *Don't Know You Don't Know* meetings—**DKDK meetings** for short.

You cannot know what will come out of such a meeting—if you did know, it wouldn't be in your blind spot. Who are the required participants at such a meeting? What should you write down for an agenda? How can you know? In fact, we can describe the concrete result that comes out of any **DKDK meeting**: it is a list of problems you didn't know you had.

In fact, these **DKDK meetings** are specially designed to bring to bear the wisdom of your entire **cross-functional project team** and to uncover hidden issues and risks—and cause action. That means representatives from every **track** of the project are required.

Another cautionary tale:

> Jackie gets her team together for a periodic status meeting. She calls it her weekly staff meeting. Her agenda states each participant will tell the boss what she's been doing for the preceding period.
>
> So they go around the room, and everyone says what they've been doing. Some give a brief summary, some go into lengthy detail (which many in the room don't understand, but that doesn't matter because they are mostly engrossed in their mobile phones).
>
> Occasionally, someone will tell the story of a problem she is having, and someone else in the room might offer an idea for a solution.

> But nobody was "on the hook" to raise issues—they were simply asked what they were doing. These issues are raised by accident.

DKDK meetings in RUF, in contrast, are set up to raise issues by design. We'll describe them in detail, but as we do, imagine going through these meetings exactly as they are designed. It may not be obvious from the descriptions that executing the meeting rigorously according to its design causes teams to surface issues in their **blind spots**. But it does.

The two **DKDK meetings** specified by RUF are the **weekly accountability meeting (WAM)** and the **definition meeting**.

These are not the only **DKDK** meetings you will have on your projects—you probably already have some that you do. For example, an effective design or code review is a **DKDK meeting**. If you are a software company, you may mandate code modules are reviewed before they are committed to the software repository. The review is designed to "catch" issues the coders were blind to. What does this mean? It means the participants should be selected to provide the kinds of background and expertise that will surface issues. That is why it is common to invite programmers from other projects and with different backgrounds and levels of experience, as well as programmers who will have to interface with or test the given module—in that context, you have a diverse set of participants who are more likely to identify problems or risks to which the presenting coders were blind.

This is not an informational meeting. How the user communicates the required "result" of this meeting to the participants is decisive: If you inform participants, "We're here to review the code," they will sit and listen to a presentation. If you tell them, "We're here to catch issues the coders were blind to," they will engage in a more active, productive, useful way. A code review is successful when it results in a list of issues that the coders need to address.

Setting Up a Meeting Room for Success

DKDK meetings are expensive, and it pays to set them up for success. This requires attention to several details that for a smaller issue-focused meeting you might let slide. Here's the physical setup we use for all our **DKDK meetings**—all of them.

Fig. 22: Setting up the room for a definition meeting.

One Room: For **DKDK meetings** to work, it is important people see and hear one another. Ideally, they should all be in one room. Our clients routinely fly remote team members to a single location for full-day **definition meetings**. The next best option is to have everyone on a video link. It is nearly impossible to make a **DKDK meeting** work over an audio conference-call line. Clear communication requires trust and relatedness; it is most reliable when people have an unimpeded channel where they can both see and hear one another. As the team uses a communication channel with lower bandwidth, the risk of misunderstanding increases, getting clear takes longer, and team members can more easily "shut down" or "hide out." Even more importantly, it is hard to see these problems occurring, so they can be detected and corrected. **DKDK** conversations, due to their exploratory nature, are particularly difficult under these circumstances.

Shared Screen: RUF meetings are designed to provoke specific conversations, but don't confuse conversations with results. As issues are identified and **action items** are assigned, these need to be written down for everyone to see in the moment. The low-tech method was to put pen to butcher paper taped to a wall, but these days, it is preferable to display a computer screen on the wall on which documents can be displayed and edited in real time. At some points in these meetings, individuals may be asked to make presentations, so their presentation materials may also go up on the shared screen. If you have multiple sites on a video conference link, they need to both see one another and see the shared screen.

Seating: Arrange the meeting chairs and tables so participants are sitting in a U shape, facing the shared screen (and video conference link, if any). Take care that nobody is sitting "outside the group" (say, against the wall). All participants are equal. As people are speaking, they can speak from their seat, stand, or move to the front of the room (e.g., if they are presenting something in detail).

Recorder: A volunteer among the participants needs to write down issues as they are raised, **action items** as they are identified, and so forth, on the shared screen. She should not capture a transcript of the conversation or even summarize what's talked about. The recorder is not "taking minutes." She needs to capture only the results: conclusions, decisions, issues raised, action items assigned, and so on. For long meetings, let different people volunteer to record, because it's harder to participate while you are recording.

Strong facilitator: The project's coach, **project leader**, or another accomplished meeting **facilitator** is charged with chauffeuring the meeting through its paces and moderating the conversations that ensue. Every meeting, but especially large rigorous meetings, can benefit from skilled facilitation. Perhaps you don't have this skill on your team, and the fact you don't have it was in your blind spot. Consider yourself unblinded—investing in good meeting facilitation makes a difference. The responsibilities of a good **facilitator** include the following:

◆ **Time management:** The team counts on the **facilitator** to call the meeting to order on time, to ensure breaks are taken during long meetings, being clear about when to reconvene, and to end the meeting at the agreed-upon time.

- **Presenting questions:** Introducing each element of the structured conversations of the meeting, asking the key questions, eliciting responses.

- **Keeping focus:** Noticing when the conversation is diverging from the goals of the meeting, and firmly interrupting such conversations to get the meeting back on track to achieve its goal.

- **Ensuring participation:** Meeting dynamics typically include those who participate a lot and those who hang back. The **facilitator** notices when some participants are quiet and pulls them into the conversation.

- **Feeding the record:** In the conversation that ensues, as the **facilitator** detects an action item has been articulated, she'll repeat it clearly for the **recorder** to capture it. She'll briefly pause the meeting to ensure it was accurately and completely captured. She may interrupt, if the action item is unclear, to push the participants to suggest language that is clearer. The **facilitator** is focused like a laser on making sure discoveries from the conversation don't get lost but get recorded so they will translate into action.

Effective Meeting Facilitation

Particularly for large, complex, or contentious meetings, the **facilitator** needs to wield a firm hand to channel conversations toward delivering the successful outcome the **owner** requires. Facilitators need to be aware of when to interrupt a conversation and when not to. For example, sometimes the team cannot focus on their goal until they get something off their chest, so best to let them have it out. Other times, the entire room will sigh with relief when the **facilitator** gently interrupts particularly indulgent, but manifestly unproductive, storytelling behavior—especially when it is the most senior manager in the room whom nobody else would be willing to interrupt.

For this to work, even with senior participants in the room, a good **facilitator** begins a meeting by stating the goal of the meeting and requesting explicit permission of all the participants to let her drive them toward that goal. This gives the **facilitator** cover to interrupt the action and get the meeting back on track when she notices a conversation (or monologue) is not moving the participants toward their goal.

DKDK meetings are fragile—the moment participants notice an issue has been revealed, like moths to a flame they will immediately derail the meeting to address that issue. But that is counter to the goal of the **DKDK** meeting, which is to *identify* issues, not resolve them. The **facilitator** wields a strong hand to stop the participants from diving directly into problem solving and to keep the meeting focused on raising issues, getting them recorded, and assigning **action items** and owners to them and then moving on. (The **owner** of the action item can, if she needs to, schedule an issue-oriented meeting limited to the required participants later.)

In addition, meeting participants will often be drawn to giving long descriptions or telling stories about their decisions, their reasoning, their experiences—it is the job of the

facilitator to notice when this strays from advancing the meeting toward accomplishing its goal and tactfully interrupt that behavior.

THINGS TO REMEMBER

◆ There must be no question who is the single, accountable, empowered project leader for any given active project. She must be on the hook for the project's successful execution.

◆ Leverage the wisdom of your entire **project team** from the beginning of your project to identify and mitigate risks you didn't even know you had. This means having a cross-functional project team from the first day of the project.

◆ The key to changing team behavior with RUF is to train your team in the small number of structures and practices that support early identification of risk, and deploy them with rigor and transparency.

CHAPTER 7

DKDK MEETINGS IN RISK UP FRONT

This chapter describes in detail the two types of **DKDK** meetings used on RUF projects: the **weekly accountability meeting** (WAM) and the **definition meeting**.

THE DEFINITION MEETING

Before the first **WAM**, the **project leader** will schedule the first of several **definition meetings**. This first meeting kicks off the project.

The **definition meeting** is one of the core practices of Risk Up Front that focuses the team on identifying and mitigating risks early in the **commitment phase**. The first one should be held within days of the start of the project.

It requires the attendance of the entire **core team** (for smaller projects, the entire project team will attend). Because it is a **DKDK** meeting designed to uncover blind spots, it is designed to be messy and expensive. Although teams are often uncomfortable when they start holding these meetings, it is because they are designed to uncover problems. These meetings end with the project having more problems, not fewer! To be precise, the problems were always there—they were simply in the team's blind spot. As teams develop their competence at engaging in **definition meetings**, they will discover this is a competitive advantage: in a world of optimistic procrastinators, this is what urgency looks like.

Out of the issues and risks the team identifies, they will create the **action items** to handle those issues and mitigate those risks *outside* the meeting. This list of **action items** is, in fact, the most important result of a **definition meeting**.

The review of the **project statement** anchors the **definition meeting**, although the other RUF **project documents** will come into play. The **project statement** communicates in no more than three pages the **target customer**, the **measures of success** (from the point of view of both the customer and the organization), and **project end date**. In other words, the Why, What, and When of the project.

The Read-Through

The **definition meeting**, although long, is simple. First, two documents are made available on the shared screen. The **recorder** will flip between them, at the direction of the **facilitator**:

- ◆ The current draft of the **project statement**, ready for review and to be updated by the team during the meeting.

- ◆ An **action item** spreadsheet, ready to display on the shared screen. For convenience, this can be a tab within the **weekly schedule** spreadsheet, initially empty, ready to receive actions that come up during the meeting. The actions can be cut and pasted onto the appropriate weekly tabs later, based on their delivery dates.

The meeting consists of an item-by-item read-through of the current draft of the **project statement**, orchestrated by the **facilitator**. For each item, the **facilitator** will have a team member read it (go around the room to keep people involved), and then she will ask the team three questions, having the team discuss each question in turn:

1. Is it clear?
2. Is it accurate?
3. Does it belong here?

As the team goes through the document item by item, they will discuss what they've written and notice things that are not clear, not correct, not appropriate, need further research, entail an acceptable or unacceptable risk, will require a person who is or a skill that is currently not present on the team, and so on. In response to these observations, the team will realize they should change what they read. They will suggest adding a word, removing a word, changing the framing, clarifying a risky ambiguity. They will also realize they need to know things they don't know—they will identify **action items** and agree to own them.

Is it clear?

The team is staring at a sentence or bullet point, and it has been read to them. Now the team needs to predict "What are all the creative ways this will be misunderstood?"

In assessing whether any statement is clear, participants will craft language that the team understands. If you are a new team member or are unfamiliar with any word or phrase in the item under discussion, perhaps because it is a bit of jargon or term of art used by this company or their products, you are obligated to say so. When the **facilitator** notices some phrase or jargon has people squirming, she pauses the conversation and makes sure it is handled. Occasionally, teams will take that opportunity to rewrite their jargon to be less obscure.

In addition, the team should consider who will read the document: for example, current team members, future new team members, managers outside the team—probably not customers. They can then assess whether the statement, as written, would be clear to that audience.

Remember, all your *spoken* explanations, discussions, details, and stories will disappear when the meeting adjourns. Future readers must understand your intentions exclusively from the words on the page—they must stand alone. Imagine someone reading your words on the **project statement**—a manager, a new teammate, or your future self a month from now after you've forgotten what you meant. If you find you have to say things to "explain" your meaning, you have lost. Keep that in mind as you are deciding whether the language in your **project statement** is clear.

Is it accurate?

When assessing accuracy, the team may notice that they really need to address an area but don't know (yet) exactly what they should say. For example, during one definition meeting read-through, a team member presented one of the **customer measures of success** that said:

```
1.  The ability to rapidly access the market
    value of their portfolio.
```

The team members raised all sorts of questions, provoking both changes to the language and **action items** to resolve issues after the meeting. For example:

◆ Rapidly? How rapidly?

◆ How would the **target customer** measure speed? In seconds? In mouse clicks? Worst case? Typical case? What is typical? Does it depend on the size of the portfolio?

◆ Would they prefer to get access in ten seconds, which we can build and deliver in one month, or two seconds, delivered in three months?

- Market value as of when? Previous end of day? Real time? Based on asset prices from the exchange that are received on a fifteen-minute delay? Is the **target customer** willing to bear the added price associated with licensing real-time data to get their portfolio value?

- What does portfolio mean? What if the **target customer** has multiple portfolios—do we support their ability to get the market value of each one?

In the above example, after discussing that one item, the team chose to rework the language of that measure in the meeting. The **facilitator** asked a team member to propose new language, the **facilitator** repeated it for the **recorder**, and the **recorder** typed it onto the live **project statement** projected on the shared screen. That one item turns into several items right there in the room:

```
1.  The ability to save, view, modify, and
    delete up to [10?] [equity?] portfolios
    containing up to [500?] positions, either
    by entering individual positions or
    uploading a properly formatted file.

2.  The ability to choose a subscription to
    either "previous end-of-day" valuation for
    [$5/month?] or "real-time" valuation for
    [$20/month?].

3.  The ability to view a web page containing
    the value of a portfolio, priced according
    to their subscription. The web page,
    including value, must fully load in under
    [5?] seconds.
```

Do you see all those question marks and brackets? Each represents a measure the team wasn't sure of, and as they recorded it during the meeting, Claire (from Sales) and Pramila (from Engineering) told the team they would take on these **action items**, which the **recorder** typed onto the action item list (also projected in front of the team):

Action Item: Propose numbers for the customer measure of success placeholders related to portfolio management, valuation, and pricing based on conversations with the target customer and with José [Product Marketing] and integrate them into the project statement.

Owner: Claire.

Deadline: next Tuesday.

Action Item: Confirm that the size of the portfolio, if it is on the order of what Claire determines, is not likely to be material in determining the maximum time to deliver a portfolio valuation.

Owner: Pramila [Engineering].

Deadline: next Friday.

Does it belong here?

Finally, the facilitator will ask whether the item is appropriate to this section of this document.

In our example of a **customer measure of success**, we expect the item to be a specific and measurable capability that the **target customer** would claim is necessary for them to buy what the team is building. Is it really? If not, further adjustments can be made, perhaps based on what participants in the room already know, or perhaps they realize they need to investigate it to deliver to the team answers they can stand behind.

Measurability is crucial. If you can't measure it, how will you know if it is done?

You might also read an item and simply conclude it doesn't belong on the project statement. Remember, you have only three pages to describe the entire project.

You might also ask, is it expressed at the right level of detail? Do we need this item to be framed more generally, to cover more ground, or at a more detailed level to mitigate high risks associated with specific details? An example of a more general expression of our example **customer measure of success** related to load time might be:

```
1.  No customer-facing web page in the system
    will take more than five seconds to load,
    under a standard user configuration (refer
    to spec document [link]).
```

If the team can stand behind a general decision like this, then a large number of individual measures (all of which must be tested, of course) need not be listed on the **project statement**.

The result of the read-through, item by item, is a revised draft **project statement**, projected in the room before the entire team, with various tentative statements and placeholders that need to be resolved, plus the **action items** to resolve them, usually with deadlines set prior to the next **definition meeting**.

Because the most important result of the **definition meeting** is the list of **action items** the team generates, we will often take the opportunity to encourage the team to generate a target number of **action items** during the read-through—for example, "Let's get ten **action items** on the board between now and lunch." Using **action items** as the measure of meeting success focuses them on uncovering new issues, and it helps to limit distracting conversations around resolving issues that have already been identified.

This three-question process is ideal for having a team review any document, any action item, and any risk entry in any meeting. It is not just for the definition meeting read-through.

The team will notice they are identifying risks that apply to the project, even while the project is partially and tentatively defined. If they can rapidly craft the cause, effect, and impact language in the room, these can be added to the **risk action plan** then and there. Otherwise, the individual who raised the risk can take on the action item to deliver a completed **risk action plan** entry by the end of the day.

The **definition meeting** is designed to be long, messy, and expensive. For projects with fewer than a dozen team members, a **definition meeting** generally takes four hours (with appropriate breaks). Larger project teams should budget a full workday. The length is intentional—it is designed to slow down and focus the team away from the problems *they know they know* and onto discovering problems in their blind spot. In fact, don't be discouraged if your first definition meeting does not get through the entire project statement. The most useful measure of success for these meetings is the list of action items they generate as issues and risks are identified.

Before teams begin using Risk Up Front, it is often unusual for them to have team-wide facilitated conversations that debate who the **target customer** should be for a new project. At first, team members may feel it is unnecessary. But when the discussion starts, and they notice their colleagues were unclear or mistaken about whom the project is for, they become believers.

DKDK meeting sessions are intentionally inefficient and may be uncomfortable. We are asking team members to question their assumptions and explicitly ensure everyone has a shared understanding of the **project definition**. High-performance teams are comfortable constantly assuming that they have yet to uncover the biggest risks on their projects. They look for new opportunities to take corrective action early in the pursuit of ensuring success.

At the First Definition Meeting

For the first **definition meeting**, the **project leader**, or the appropriate **track lead**, may write down her best guess at who the **target customer** and what the **measures of success** are. But we encourage project leaders to tread lightly—consider starting the project with a **project statement** draft that does little more than reflect the opportunity and give the team the flexibility to fill it out, so they can arrive at the tradeoff that best exploits that opportunity. They'll begin by noticing all the things they don't know, and this will generate the initial set of **action items** that will start the team working.

Here are examples of typical **action items** that come out of early **definition meetings**:

♦ You may assign someone to craft language for a specific part of the **project statement**, such as describing the **business measures** for the project, or research and update a **customer measure of success** or **component**.

♦ You may add a newly identified risk to the **risk action plan** so the risk's **owner** can get into action on mitigating it.

♦ You may ask representatives from multiple tracks to meet offline and resolve a tradeoff, then propose new language for the **project statement**.

♦ It is common to realize the project needs to accomplish something no one on the current team can accomplish. You may assign someone to go out and find a person (hire? transfer? train?) to join the team and own that deliverable.

♦ You may identify someone to do some scheduling (or organize the creation of a schedule) out of which can come a tentative **project end date**.

Activity during the **commitment phase** is focused on clarifying what the project needs to be and identifying and mitigating risks sufficiently so the team's **commitment** to deliver it successfully is robust. All other activity should be postponed until the **delivery phase**.

The **project leader**, as a rule of thumb, will schedule three to five definition meetings over what she expects to be the first quarter (or so) of the project timeline. For any moderately complex project, it generally takes this long to do enough research, perform enough experiments, and secure enough of the right resources to ensure the resulting project definition is both valuable and worthy of their **commitment**. Those meetings don't need to all be scheduled on day one, but you do need to account for the lead time required to get the **core team** together and the facilities set up. Leave enough time between **definition meetings** to complete the **action items** that have been identified as required to unblock **commitment**.

Midway through the **commitment phase**, invite the entire **project team** (including any members who are not on the core team) to participate in a **definition meeting**. You will need their **commitment**, and you want to hear their concerns and perspective during the commitment phase to identify risks.

At the Last Definition Meeting

The last **definition meeting** ends when the read-through is complete without the team identifying any remaining issues or unmitigated risks that stand in the way of their **commitment**. The team should expect that the **project statement** and the composition of the **project team** are frozen. The **project leader** asks each team member whether she can commit to deliver the project as described, and if everyone says, "Yes, even in the face of circumstances," the **definition meeting** is over, and the **commitment phase** is concluded.

You can't be sure at the start of any definition meeting if it is going to be the last one.

Because the design of the **definition meeting** is to identify **blind spots**, you can't know in advance that you have (given diligent probing) found the last one you're going to find.

In practice, the team will assemble for what is expected to be the last **definition meeting**. There will be a read-through, and everyone is ready to commit except for one or two outstanding issues. The team will decide it needs one or two more days to resolve them, and the meeting ends. After a few days, the team is brought together and agrees the last few issues are resolved. Everyone then commits, signs the **project statement**, and celebrates with pizza or ice cream.

During the **commitment phase**, the focus of your **definition meetings** will evolve:

- ♦ Early **definition meetings** are focused on risk identification and uncovering **blind spots**—mitigation begins immediately.

- ♦ Midway through the **commitment** phase, **definition meetings** are focused on exploring **tradeoffs**.

- ♦ The remaining **definition meetings** are focused on confirming that the project definition is clear, accurate, and represents precisely what the team is committed to achieve.

THE WEEKLY ACCOUNTABILITY MEETING

Every project, as soon as it is approved to begin, will set aside one hour a week for the **core team** to meet for a **weekly accountability meeting (WAM)**. This meeting sets a rhythm of establishing **transparency** and **integrity** on your project from the beginning.

The **WAM** revolves around a RUF **project document** called the **weekly schedule**. It is a spreadsheet document with multiple tabs (i.e., individual spreadsheets), one tab per WAM. On the tab for a given WAM are listed all the deliverables team members committed to be completed by that WAM. Think of it as one "page" per week.

The basic idea of the **WAM** is to create a weekly rhythm of "commit and deliver." The **weekly schedule**, across all its weekly tabs, contains all the commitments the project must track to end successfully. The team achieves 100 percent success on the project by achieving 100 percent on its **weekly schedule**.

The purpose of the WAM is to cause *100 percent complete* in the coming week.

Don't get derailed. The **WAM** is not the place to review the history of activity on the project or the status of tasks (other than **done/not done**).

The **WAM** uncovers **blind spots** by doing four exercises, in order:

1. **Establish Done/Not Done:** Clearly state before the entire team which of the deliverables committed to be done by this **WAM** (due this week, listed on this tab) are in fact done and which are not done. Limit your assessment to the deliverables written on this week's list (other stuff may have gotten done, ignore that for the moment).

2. **Report Weekly Percent Complete:** Report to the team (and record) the **weekly percent complete**. This is simply the ratio of **weekly deliverables** you reported as "done" divided by the number of **weekly deliverables** on the list (i.e., that were committed to be done by this **WAM**). It represents the fraction of the recorded commitments for the past week that were accomplished.

3. **Confirm commitment:** Review the "not done" items and make the appropriate adjustments to future **action items** on the **weekly schedule** to account for them. Review the items due by the next **WAM**, those listed on the next tab, and have each item's **owner** confirm she stands by her **commitment** to get it done. Determine if any future milestones are now at risk, and define action items to resolve any issues.

4. **Risk transparency:** Go around the room and have each team member answer the precise question, "What are the top two risks that you believe will cause the project to fail?"

As you are stepping through the **WAM**, measure **accountability**, **transparency**, **integrity**, and **commitment** with rigor. One important tool for this is to consistently pose questions that address these four principles without fail:

- **Transparency:** Is the done/not-done state of each action item inarguably clear? Hint: If it's not clear, it may be you don't know what happened. However, it is equally common that the action item is ambiguous, and different people have different opinions about what "done" means. As you record **action items** on the **weekly schedule**, you want the entire team to continuously check what they have written for clarity.

- **Accountability:** Is there confusion about who owns what? Do you think you are being held accountable for something you shouldn't be? Are you unable to deliver on your accountabilities because of something else going on in your world, conflicts, emergencies?

- **Integrity:** If something is marked "done," is it completely "done"? If we say we are committed to deliver an action item for next week, are we committed to deliver exactly the thing that is written down? Do we need to adjust or refine what we wrote?

- **Commitment:** When reviewing what is to be delivered by the next **WAM**, are we in fact committed as in "It will be so, even in the face of circumstances"? Are there any risky dependencies on which your **commitment** depends? Surface those and deal with them before committing.

We suggest project teams schedule their **WAM** in the middle of the week so there are workdays both immediately before and after the **WAM** for team members to scramble to get their **action items** done on time.

We also suggest teams set aside an hour. In the beginning, getting through the four agenda items may take the full hour, but in our experience, even large teams on complex projects, after a few attempts, can get the whole meeting done in twenty or thirty minutes. The remaining time can be used for activities relevant to the entire **project team**, such as presenting project results, doing a demo, or working on the mitigation of a risk that involves many functional groups.

Often, there is a risk or issue that has been identified that requires urgent action by a subset of the **WAM** attendees. In that case, have the smaller group hold that working meeting immediately after the **WAM** is complete, and let everyone else leave early. The practice of having team members block out the full hour allows the right people to be ready and available for urgent action without having to wait for the follow-up meeting to be scheduled.

Let's now look closer at the four parts of the **WAM**:

1. Establishing done/not done
2. Reporting the weekly percent complete
3. Confirming commitment
4. Risk transparency

Establish Done/Not Done

When we ask teams to write down their **action items** and then later assess whether they were delivered, the first thing they often notice is they have to argue about whether something is done or not. They will tell complicated stories about why something is not done, or how the important bit is done and the rest doesn't matter, or how it is almost completely done, and the rest will be done by the end of the day. In other words, they notice how bad they are at wording **action items**, so they capture, at the right level, the valuable result that needs to be achieved in words that are sufficiently unambiguous. This must eliminate argument, after the fact, whether the action item is done.

The **project leader** must know the done/not-done status of every deliverable that is listed on this week's schedule tab *prior to the WAM*. It is a complete waste of time to ask around and figure that out during the meeting. If you own an action item that is due today, take responsibility for making sure the **project leader** knows prior to the meeting if it is done or not done. You don't need to explain or tell a story; just be clear about what is so. Your team may set a ground rule saying, for example, that deliverable owners must give their done/not-done status to the **project leader** by the end of the day prior to each **WAM**.

Report Weekly Percent Complete

Because the **project leader** knows the state of each of this week's **action items** prior to the **WAM**, she also knows the

weekly percent complete. These should be recorded on the **weekly schedule** tab prior to the meeting so it is displayed to the team at the start of the meeting.

Why do we insist that we account weekly for the percent complete? It is based on the principle of **accountability**: you get what you measure. If you measure each week whether the team has achieved 100 percent, then the team will work to achieve 100 percent.

We commonly see in the first meeting, that the **weekly percent complete** is embarrassingly low, and then teams get their act together. Teams become more careful in considering what they commit to and what risks stand in their way—their **commitment** thus becomes more robust. They will also push to get the last few items done for the week. A few late nights early in the project will prevent working on the weekends later in the schedule.

Remember that the **weekly percent complete** measures the **integrity** of the team *as a team*. When used properly, it begins to foster a culture where all the team members hold themselves accountable for the team hitting 100 percent each week. It is not about "I got my stuff done; why couldn't you get yours done?" Putting this dynamic into the culture of your teams is one of the most powerful ingredients for creating high performance.

Obviously, the **weekly percent complete** is an imperfect measure, and yet it is incredibly useful. Think of it like a warning light in your car. When the light goes on, it may mean that you need more windshield wiper fluid, or it can mean that the engine is about to fall out. You may not know which one it is, but that light forces you to stop and ask the question. In RUF, we are using the weekly percent complete as a proxy for how well your team is performing. We are measuring **integrity**. A low score may simply be a result of the flu going around the office that week, or it may represent a fundamental problem in the organization of your project. A low score should trigger an inquiry. The simplicity of the arithmetic helps make it wonderfully transparent. It is a powerful practice that reveals issues in the team's blind spot throughout the project.

> Here is a practice that many of our clients find useful: If the team measures 60 percent complete or below on a given week, or 80 percent complete or below two weeks in a row, then, the day after the WAM, the project leader should have a mini-review with senior management. Management needs to consider there may be structural problem on the project they need to address, such as resource issues or fundamental technical problems.
>
> We like to say, "If the team is hitting below 80 percent two weeks in a row, shame on the team. If it's hitting below 80 percent four weeks in a row, then shame on management."

Occasionally, teams will come back to us saying, "Well, the important stuff got done." We want to be clear that the entire team and management are trusting you to deliver on all the commitments you make. That is why the **weekly percent complete** does not weight accomplishments (or lack thereof) by importance. It is a measure of the team's ability to keep its word.

Confirm Commitment

In this section, we consider whether something that is **not done** is important or not. We need to determine what is the right thing to do in the face of it having not been done. There are a couple of obvious possibilities:

- **Can we simply commit to a new date?** It may still be an important thing to get done, so we should confirm the **owner** still owns it (reassigning it if necessary) and ask her what date she can commit to. This results in the action item being copied and pasted to a future schedule tab.

- **When will it happen?** It may be the **owner** is unable to commit to the result because she needs to mitigate some risks, handle some dependencies, or solve some intervening problem. This may result in several new **action items**, which can, in the room, be assigned owners and committed dates. It is acceptable for the **owner** to do some research after the meeting and give a committed date to the **project leader** by the end of the day.

- **What else may slip?** It may be that other **action items** that depend on the "not done" one will slip, or it may be possible to squeeze things in so they remain intact. Right after the **WAM**, the **owner** should gather the owners of dependent **action items** and confirm they are still committed, or identify what adjustments they need to make to their commitments and get them to the **project leader** by the end of the day.

- **Do we still need it?** It may be that the team realizes they didn't need that result after all, and nothing needs to be added or changed on future **action items**.

To make this section of the meeting go rapidly, it is important to allow only minimal "problem solving"—don't let the conversation go off the rails. Because the **WAM** is a **DKDK** meeting, you want all the participants to recognize that the *discovery* that something is an issue is valuable. If it is obvious and uncomplicated how to change the **weekly schedule** to address a "not done" item (e.g., "Oops, sorry, I'll get it done in the next hour"), go ahead and address it then and there. If it requires more analysis, get the right team members together immediately after the **WAM** to figure it out and update the schedule by the end of the day.

After the schedule has been adjusted, review next week's committed items. Read through each one and have the **owner** confirm she is committed to deliver that result prior to the next **WAM**. If, while reading through the list, you notice some result is not clear, or not exactly right, or not appropriate, adjust it then and there if you can do so quickly. As teams become proficient running the WAM, they will often take this opportunity to review and confirm commitment to deliverables two to three weeks out.

No later than the end of the day of the **WAM**, the **project leader** should have clear commitments by identified owners to deliver clearly identified results by the next **WAM**.

Risk Transparency

After the team has committed to next week's results, the **project leader** poses this question to the team:

> "What, in your opinion, are the top two risks that will cause this project to fail?"

The **facilitator** will then call on each person in turn, going around the room, and every team member will answer that question.

Team members, at the beginning, will work hard to *do this wrong*. We often hear individuals answer some different question; for example, they may inadvertently answer the following:

♦ "What are the risks in my area?"
♦ "What are two new risks that that are not on the list?"
♦ "What am I obsessively worried about, although if it happens, I don't think it will cause the project to fail?"

The **facilitator** needs to detect and correct that and make sure each team member answers the question precisely.

> "What are the top two risks that will cause this project to fail?"

Let's also be clear that we are not asking, "Does anyone have any risks?" One of the most magical dynamics of the risk transparency ritual is we are making the sharing of everyone's top two risks *mandatory*. It is part of the definition of what it means to be a team member.

Keep in mind there is always an answer to the question, *"What are the top two risks that will cause this project to fail?"* At some point, a team member may feel things are so "under control" that her top risk may be, say, that the team is located on an earthquake fault, so there may be an earthquake that will delay the project. If that really is the biggest risk to your project, then say so. It suggests you are doing well. In practice, we rarely hear about the earthquake risk—if you're working on, say, physical infrastructure, though, you might.

Every team member knows in advance of the **WAM** that the "top risks" question is going to be asked, and teams that do their **WAM** efficiently come prepared—they have written down their top two risks before the meeting, and unless something came up in the **WAM** that changes their opinion, they simply read what they wrote so the entire team can hear it.

On projects where team members attend the WAM remotely, via phone or video-conference, our clients often find it useful for members to submit their risks on a slide in advance of the meeting. They share those slides during the risk transparency conversation so everyone can see the top two risks while each team member is reading aloud what they wrote. This is particularly helpful when there are non-native English speakers.

Newbies will sometimes accompany their written top risk answer with long explanations of why they picked that risk, stories about why it is important, and so on. The **facilitator** will gently interrupt, then ask them to read what they wrote. This has two beneficial effects. First, they are on notice that their written words need to be clear and precise enough to stand on their own (later, readers of the **risk action plan** won't have the luxury of hearing any accompanying oral explanations). Second, the **WAM** won't take as long.

It is not important that the mentioned risks are unique or novel. It is useful information for a team to hear multiple individuals articulate similar risks.

For each team member, after their risks have been articulated, the **project leader** will note if that risk already exists on the

risk action plan (chapter 3). If not, she will ask the team member to craft the wording of her risk and submit it by the end of the day for inclusion in the **risk action plan**.

If the same risk is raised in multiple **WAMs**, that is a red flag that the team is not effectively getting into action to mitigate that risk (or not effectively communicating that the risk has been mitigated). Because these risks may be fatal to the project, the risk's **owner** may need to escalate to get the resources (or creativity) to mitigate it promptly, either by reducing the probability of the effect or removing the cause.

THINGS TO REMEMBER

♦ The **weekly accountability meeting** and **definition meeting** are "Don't know what you don't know" meetings. They are designed to identify hidden issues and confirm team assumptions so issues are revealed sooner. They are expensive, inefficient, and sometimes uncomfortable. High-performance teams learn to get great at them.

♦ The purpose of the **definition meeting** is to identify new issues and actions and move the team to a committed definition. It requires full participation of the core team. Reschedule the meeting if **core team** members are missing.

♦ The objective of the **weekly accountability meeting** is to set up the next week for "100 percent **done**" and leverage the cross-functional **core team** to identify and cause action on critical risks continuously through the entire life of the project.

♦ Move conversations offline (by recording an **action item**) as soon as an issue is identified in a **DKDK** meeting. Don't have ten people watch two people commandeering your meeting to resolve their problem.

CHAPTER 8

RUF PROJECT DOCUMENTS:
MANAGING TO FOUR SHEETS OF PAPER

Projects are full of documents—specs, designs, code, plans, schedules, user stories, contracts, documentation, and so on. What documents you need depends both on what your project is trying to accomplish and perhaps also on your organizational project governance. For example, if you are building devices subject to regulatory control, there may be regulations that specify what you document.

Your organization may already have templates or processes for generating, sharing, maintaining, getting sign-offs or approvals, archiving, and controlling such documents. Or it may not.

Regardless, for projects large and small, on top of whatever documents your project requires, RUF projects develop and center their work on four simple documents: the **project statement**, the **team list** with **individual accountabilities**, the **weekly schedule**, and the **risk action plan**. We've used this simple approach on projects ranging from the simple and small to complex projects involving hundreds of team members spread

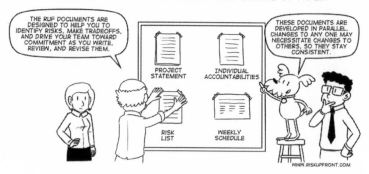

Fig. 23: Managing your project using four sheets of paper.

in subteams around the world. We will talk about some ways of adapting these tools to large projects in part 3, but for many projects, this may be all the organizational scaffolding your project needs.

This chapter describes these project documents in detail. You will find complete examples in the appendix, and both examples and templates can be downloaded at https://www.riskupfront.com.

Taken together, these four RUF **project documents**, at the end of the **commitment phase**, will transparently convey the **5W tradeoff** the team has identified—one that they are committed to achieve and that management is willing to fund:

- ◆ **Why** the project is being undertaken for an explicit opportunity and customer

- ◆ **What** capabilities are created for the customer who buys what the project built, what the team will build to get those results into the customer's hands, and what business results (profit) the organization expects to gain from that

♦ **Who** are the team members accountable for building whatever needs to be built

♦ **When** is the deadline by which the results will be completed

♦ **Why not**—the team is taking this on in the face of what risks

THE LIFE OF PROJECT DOCUMENTS

When you decide to begin your project, you may have nothing but an opportunity and an assigned **project leader** with a decision to invest resources in defining a project. At that point, you can create all the RUF **project documents** and put them in your project folder. But of course, they'll be mostly empty, because you do not know what the project is yet.

Over the life of your project, these documents will be edited and will evolve. We recommend you maintain them under revision control—for example, in your version control system or in a versioned document repository, such as Google Docs.

The State of the Document

There are two types of project documents. The first type is used to settle and communicate decisions: your document begins in draft form, and through discussion and research, it evolves into its final form—it describes the decisions the team has made. The other type describes "what is so" on the project, and as the project progresses, these documents are updated to describe the current state of the project. Thus, documents are in one of three states:

♦ **Draft:** The claims the document makes are tentative, hypothetical, incomplete, and under discussion by the team. They are not decisions.

♦ **Final:** The claims the document makes have been committed to by the team and are not expected to change. The document asserts decisions.

♦ **Current (as of):** The document is a living document to be modified periodically over the life of the project. Such a document should be labeled, "Current as of [date]." You can imagine printing it out, picking it up a month later, and being perfectly clear as to what it represents: the state of the project as of that date.

Get used to the fact that documents get printed out, passed around, forwarded among managers and others outside the team, and so on. Get in the habit of marking your documents loudly at the top to identify what state they are in so readers don't get confused as to whether the claims in the document represent guesses or decisions. This is a good practice for any document on your project (e.g., specs, plans, etc.). It is important to share drafts, but do not mislead readers into thinking they represent decisions until they do.

It's also a good practice to write at the top of all your project documents the name and contact information of the documents' **owner** (the individual who is accountable for its integrity). The RUF **project documents** are generally owned by the **project leader**. For large projects, the **project leader** will delegate this **accountability** to the person who has been assigned the role of maintaining all the project documents (e.g., a project librarian or similar role).

Tentative Claims and Placeholders in Drafts

As project documents evolve, teams often find they write down the things they know about (or are sure of) and are silent on the areas where they don't know the answers. Perhaps they don't want to address an issue lest anyone reading the document think they've decided when they haven't (yet).

Don't do that. While RUF **project documents** are in the DRAFT state, of course you'll be writing down your best guess as to what they should contain. But if you clearly mark your document as DRAFT, you can, and should, also include tentative claims and placeholders. This allows the team to gather the list of things they know they need to include, without having to do the work necessary to make final decisions on those things. We like to use [brackets] to mark these:

- **Tentative claims:** Statements you are not sure are true—enclose them in [brackets] to indicate tentative language or suffix them with "[?]" to indicate they need to be checked or confirmed.

- **Placeholders:** Sometimes you know you need to make some sort of claim about a thing but don't know (yet) what that claim should be. Use brackets to indicate what you're looking for, or what your guess is.

Placeholders can be used to separate what's known from what's not known (yet). For example, if you are building a car, and you are not sure if acceleration should be one of your **measures of success**, you might have a sentence in your draft **project statement** at some point that says

```
The ability to accelerate 0-60 mph in 6
seconds. [?]
```

But if you know you need to make a claim about acceleration, and you know you will measure acceleration as the number of seconds it takes to go 0–60 mph, but you're not certain how much your car should have, you might write in your draft something to make it clear the only tentative bit is the number of seconds.

```
The ability to accelerate 0-60 mph in [6]
seconds.
```

We find this is a succinct way to convey a great deal of information of where the team is in the process of developing their draft. Each tentative statement or placeholder in a draft is a call to action, to do what is required to settle that tentative claim into a decision. **Each tentative claim should be tied to one or more action items in the weekly schedule to ensure they get resolved.**

Concurrent and Iterative

As the team is going through its **commitment phase**, we are often asked, "Which document do we write first?" And the answer, in our experience, is, "All of them!"

The way it looks is all the RUF **project documents** are created at the same time as drafts, and they all start out roughly empty or with a few tentative statements. Then, over the course of the **commitment phase**, all the documents evolve, and based on the changes in one, teams realize they need to make changes in another as they define their project.

The writing of these project documents is concurrent (all at the same time) and iterative—each document is drafted, full of placeholders and hypotheses, and then the team goes back and updates them all, adjusting to close holes and make decisions, and then again, closing still more holes, and making and revisiting decisions until the team has settled on a set of decisions that identify a **project definition**, a **5W tradeoff**, they can commit to.

THE RUF PROJECT STATEMENT

The RUF **project statement** is a document no more than three pages long that captures the **why**, **what**, and **when** of the project. It consists of five parts, as can be seen in the **project statement** template.

```
Project {Project Name}
Project Statement
Status: {DRAFT}          Maximum 3 pages!
One-Liner:
Typically: "For X (or because of X), we will
build Y by date Z."
```

Target Customer:

For example: Individual name or demographic category. How would they describe themselves, independently of this project? Are they primary or secondary customers?

Customer Measures of Success:

To be written:
What ability or criteria will we cause, in the language of the customer, specific and measurable!

. . .

Business Measures:

To be written:
What business results will we achieve for us to consider this project a success?

ROI? How much revenue? How much profit? Over what time frame? What is the cost of being late?

Also, what is the cap on what we'll spend and the deadline by which we'll commit to being done?

Components:

To be written:
The big blocks of what we'll deliver. "What's in the box."

Covers all areas of the product experience visible to the customer or necessary for its operation, not just the technical piece.

. . .

Why is the **project statement** crucial?

The **project statement** and process by which it is developed are designed to channel the team's behavior in ways that shift the identification and mitigation of risks to the **commitment phase**.

The *process* of making it is more valuable than the resulting document. This is not a document that one person writes, then the rest of the team agrees to it. It is drafted, reviewed, adjusted, pushed, and pulled into shape by the entire team over an extended period, punctuated by hard meetings involving the entire team. The team is not expected to look at a **project statement** and say, "This seems reasonable." They are expected to change it until they've turned it into something that "will be so."

The project statement must be kept short so the entire team, and management, can anchor themselves to it, and so it can be read by the team in definition meetings.

It is brief, and that makes it usable. You cannot expect anyone—any manager, any new team member—to read a fifty-page "requirements document" to understand what you are trying to accomplish. That is not to say such a long document should or shouldn't be written—that depends on the project. But what we know is a fifty-page document is simply unworkable for effectively and transparently conveying what the team is deciding to be accountable for in language that allows management to hold the team accountable.

Project leaders love the fact that when a new team member comes on board, they can simply hand the new member a three-page document and say, "Read this," instead of meeting with them to talk through at length what the project is about.

The key to a good **project statement** is it says everything about the project's success that needs to be said, subject to the constraint that anyone—a manager, a team member, or someone newly joining the team—should be able to read it and understand the **why, what,** and **when** of the project.

Individual Sections

Project Name

Every project needs a name, and the name the team has chosen for this project is at the top of the **project statement**. This might be settled at the start of the first **definition meeting**, or the **project leader** might propose it. Finding names people like is hard—don't let it spin out of control.

What makes a good project name? In our experience, it is important *not* to name the project after what it's about. For example, if you name your refrigerator development project "The Refrigerator Project," then in hallway conversations and around the water coolers, when people mention the project by name to people who aren't on the team, outsiders will *think* they know what the project is about and make assumptions. It is also confusing if you are a refrigerator company and have several refrigerator projects going on simultaneously—people won't know which one you're referring to.

By contrast, if you give your project an opaque code name, such as "Project Tiger," instead of making assumptions about what is in scope and what is not in scope for your project, they'll ask. We suppose if your project is to deliver the next release of a product, you could name it "[Product Name] Version [X]," but that's boring, and nobody will like the T-shirts or coffee mugs you give out to the team to build their esprit de corps.

A good way to pick a project name is for the **project leader** to get a small group of people together, throw up names on a whiteboard for twenty minutes, and then have each person vote for her top three. The one with the most votes wins.

Project One-Liner

This is the elevator pitch for your project. In one to three carefully crafted sentences, it summarizes the **why**, **what**, and **when** of the project. It often has the following form:

```
Because of [Opportunity X], we will build
[Product Z] by date [project end date].
```

Or for some projects, it might look like this:

```
To enable [Customer X] to do [Y], we will
build [Z] by date [project end date].
```

The **project one-liner** is the first thing on your **project statement**, but it is the *last thing you write*. Don't spend much time on this in your first or second definition meeting. Once you've settled what the project is, then you can easily craft a good elevator pitch.

Because it needs to be short and compelling, every word must carry a lot of weight. Before the team gets around to crafting their one-liner, the team should have a good idea of what the most important aspects of the project results are—the ones they must make sure are communicated here. Sometimes adding a single adjective makes all the difference.

Target Customer

> **Customer:** The one who pays the bill. The customer is not always the user of your product.

In this section, the team describes whom they are doing this project for. The **target customer** describes who will buy what you are making, and out of sales to these customers, you will achieve the business results that are (separately) described below.

Descriptions of target customers take two forms: if you are building something for a named buyer (or set of them), list them here by name. If you are selling into a demographic (either of people or of organizations), then describe them.

Describe the **target customer** as they would describe themselves, in language that has nothing to do with your project or company. You'll notice the customer, when asked to describe themselves, would not say anything about what you are making. These are some good framing questions:

♦ How does the customer describe themselves?

♦ What is important or distinctive about the **target customer** that distinguishes them from those who are not your targets (independently of their relationship to your product)?

Your goal is to select the narrowest customer target that allows you to achieve the business results you require. As you are figuring out how to describe your **target customer**, there is the temptation to say, in effect, "The **target customer** is anyone who can use this thing I'm building." That is not workable (also, it is not how any customer would describe themselves). It is a cliché that "The product designed to satisfy everybody, satisfies nobody, and never gets shipped."

It is often crucial to distinguish between **primary target customer** and **secondary target customer** categories. Several of our clients have remarked this distinction, given the conversations and discoveries it provokes, has saved many of their projects. The primary customer is defined to be the customer you would change your design to satisfy. For a secondary customer, while you'll sell to them to achieve your business results, you explicitly decline to alter your design (**measures of success**, **components**) to address their concerns. Projects have been saved by noticing they can move a customer from the "primary" to the "secondary" category.

> **Primary target customer:** We will adjust our design to satisfy them.
>
> **Secondary target customer:** We will not adjust our design to satisfy them.

The description of the **target customer** should start with, "Who is paying the bill?" but you may need to include the end users. You must understand who these users are and how their satisfaction contributes to your customer's satisfaction.

For example, suppose you are creating a gaming technology you will license to Nintendo for inclusion in one of its products. In this example, Nintendo may be the paying customer, but the end user may be, say, "Males in the United States and China aged twelve to seventeen." If those users are not satisfied, Nintendo will not be satisfied. It is perfectly appropriate to record this understanding in the **target customer** section.

Customer Measures of Success

Imagine your **target customer** told you what they needed your project results to allow them to do for them to consider what you built to be worth buying. These are your **customer measures of success**. These do not describe what you are building; they describe what those results enable in the form of a bullet list of concise, carefully crafted descriptions. For example, if you are building a new model of automobile for a particular **target customer**, customer measures like these might appear on your **project statement**:

1. Ability to accelerate from 0 to 60 mph in 6 seconds

2. Ability to travel 40 MPG on 86 octane unleaded gasoline

3. Passes smog certification test in California

Notice each of these descriptions is specific and measurable. There is a test you can perform to determine if, in the car you build, these capabilities are present, or they are not. Notice the specificity of the circumstances: not just 40 MPG but 40 MPG given a specified quality of gasoline.

The customer does not and should not care, for the most part, what you build into the car to get it to deliver 40 MPG. In fact, we intentionally separate the conversations regarding "what the results need to achieve to satisfy the **target customer**" from "what you decide to build." The point, obviously, is to give the team maximum flexibility in choosing what to design and build, so long as they satisfy the **customer measures of success**. This is an important consideration to keep in mind, especially for the sales team, product management, and senior management: don't overspecify before involving the engineers. Give them as much design freedom as you can during the **commitment phase**.

Good measures are generally as follows:

- **Customer-centric:** Things the customer cares about, in language the customer would use. Things the customer would measure.
- **Capabilities:** What is enabled by your result, not what you are building. Customer measures of success often begin with the phrase, "Provide the ability to..."
- **Specific:** They refer to a single capability, in a carefully circumscribed context.
- **Measurable:** Both what the customer would measure (e.g., MPG) and what the resulting measurement must be to satisfy the customer (e.g., 40).
- **Necessary:** Without achieving this measure, the result is not a success; the customer would not be satisfied.

The **customer measures of success** you list should cover all aspects of your outcomes the customer would care about. For a car, the customer needs to be satisfied with the performance, the color, and the amenities, but she also needs to be satisfied with the warranty, the maintainability, the safety, the durability, and ease of purchasing. Think broadly about what will stand in the way of your customer's satisfaction, and craft customer measures that respond to those concerns.

Each **customer measure of success** in the list must be necessary for the satisfaction of the customer. Additionally, the measures, taken together, must also be sufficient.

The fact that the customer measures are both necessary and sufficient for the satisfaction of the **target customer** means that the list cannot be a "wish list" of features. It is the minimal set necessary to achieve customer satisfaction and achieve the desired business results.

It is common for teams to include in their **customer measures of success** references to a rule, standard, or credential: "Complies with California emission regulations," "Conforms to NTSB safety level 3," "UL approved." This is an efficient way to communicate exact criteria against which a deliverable can be tested. At other points, the team may decide to look inside a standard or inside a spec (such as a customer requirements document) and pull out a detail they want to highlight, because it is risky or unexpected. It is important not to feel constrained by a hierarchy of details—in some areas, the measure may be abstract (e.g., car acceleration), and in other areas, it may be a lower level detail.

In making the decision of what should be included in the **project statement**, the team should consider measures that are clearly "must-haves" to the customer and will dominate the sales conversation. Those measures may be related to "sales blockers," specs that you know will need to be met to close sales. They may be capabilities that are important differentiators. You may also want to include items that could prove controversial or unexpected both inside and outside the team just to clearly communicate what has been committed. Similarly, you may choose to include measures related to characteristics that are new or unfamiliar to the organization. By including controversial items, you may usefully provoke debate that will reveal new risks and issues.

As your team reads through the **customer measures of success**, take the opportunity to notice if some key area has been left out, particularly one that could impact customer satisfaction. That is a common mistake. Take advantage of the breadth of your **project team** to identify those missing measures. For example, ask yourself, "What do we need to deliver to the customer beyond the device itself?" Non-technical issues that impact customer satisfaction are often overlooked. Did you remember to include success criteria related to customer service? Warranty coverage? Installation experience? Sales process? Remember, your goal is not to build a widget but to satisfy a customer—these issues are integral to your project's success. Manage them with the same rigor you use for engineering.

Business Measures

These consist of another list of measures for the project but, in this case, from the point of view of your organization. Organizations use various criteria to determine how valuable their project results are. For example, businesses might use return on investment, projected profit, quantity sold, gross margin, time to obsolescence, or market share captured, to name a few. A nonprofit might use "number of clients served" or similar.

This section also includes the cost side of the equation—for example, the cost of resources required to build, the "cost of goods sold" or operating cost, projected warranty costs, some items related to the **cost of being late**, and so forth.

The **project end date** is also included in this section. Of course, while the **commitment phase** is in progress, the **project statement** is marked "DRAFT," and this date is a tentative estimate—put it in brackets! It only becomes a committed date when the team is committed to achieving the entire **5W tradeoff** (at the end of the **commitment phase**). After that, management can count on it.

Whereas the **customer measures of success** are confirmed to be true at the end of the project, many of the **business measures** become true only *after* the project ends. For example, we typically won't know if we have met our goal for "profit" at the end of the project. By including it in the **business measures**, we're saying this profit is planned. The organization should subsequently measure and confirm whether that profit is achieved. The important point is that the other aspects of the project, what is being built, and for whom are *consistent* with the projected profit and other business measures. Be sure to include both linear and nonlinear **costs of being late** in this section.

In fact, during the **delivery phase** of the project, the team should invent specific *milestones* that will confirm the project is on track to deliver a result that will achieve the desired business goals. These may include pilot tests, rounds of customer feedback, market analyses, and so on.

Components

This list describes what will be built to cause the **customer measures of success** to come true. Whereas the customer measures describe what will be true for the customer to be satisfied, the **components** list represents the decisions the team is making on how these needs will be satisfied. Think of it like the "packing list" for the box the project results come in.

The **components** should be focused on the important choices the team is making. To continue our automobile example, to achieve the acceleration that the customer requires, a component might be:

```
1.  A V8 internal combustion engine with a
    displacement of [xx] cc's

2.  A gross weight of [xx] tons

3.  A type [27-2356B] aluminum chassis
```

The list of components should be necessary and sufficient to deliver precisely the customer measures that were specified.

Because the customer measures cover all aspects of the project results that impact customer satisfaction, the components list will similarly cover all those aspects. For example:

- A warranty contract
- A user manual
- A dealership repair manual

It is often interesting to explicitly name vendor product choices for components. For example:

```
1.  Windshield Carlite #327B or equivalent
```

The Hierarchy of Context

Think of the **project statement**, using its five sections, as articulating a clear hierarchy of context. It starts with your customers. This is the dog that should wag the tail. If you get this part wrong, then the rest of the **project statement** will be incorrect, and the project will fail. You might build exactly what you said you'd build, but you won't be able to sell it.

Choosing your customers leads you to ask the question, "Given these customers, what are the criteria we must meet to have them consider themselves satisfied?"

That, then, provides a context for deciding what must be built—to meet the criteria, to satisfy the customer.

The decision to build those things entails cost, and the project needs to be "worth it." It is in the context of what you're building and for whom that you'll identify its value. That is how you establish and validate your **business measures**.

Fig. 24: The hierarchy of context for customer satisfaction.

As you debate and settle each section, your team proceeds down this hierarchy of context, from customer to need to solution to value. But be aware that every step down this hierarchy creates an opening for mistranslation and loss of fidelity. For example, you might accidentally ascribe a need incorrectly to the customer or select an inappropriate solution in the face of an ambiguous or nonexistent need. Therefore, it is critical to deploy your resources up front, deliberately, expensively, and proactively to minimize the risk of getting this wrong. The job of your team and **commitment phase** is to inspect, question, and experiment in the name of reducing the translation error. This is the soul of the Risk Up Front **commitment phase**.

How the Project Statement Gets Written

The **project leader** is accountable for causing the creation, revision, and team commitment to the **project statement**. The initial draft should be created using the above template within days of beginning the **commitment phase**. It should incorporate the latest thinking on all the sections. Like the draft **team list**, all you know is that the **project statement** is "incorrect," but you just don't know in what way yet. That's what an empowered and accountable team will sort out in the **commitment phase**, starting with the first **definition meeting**.

It is a good idea to establish clearly who is the team member who knows most about the **target customer**, who owns the customer relationship, and is best positioned to be accountable for ensuring the customer will be satisfied by the results of this project. It might be the team member from Marketing or perhaps the one from Sales. They can be charged with crafting the initial draft language for the **project statement**'s **target customer** and **customer measures of success**. Such a draft will, at least, contain placeholders for likely measures, identifying what areas might need to be covered. There will likely also be draft language about what, approximately, the **business measures** should be. The **project leader** can incorporate these into the **project statement** prior to the first **definition meeting**.

At the first **definition meeting**, an item-by-item read-through of the **project statement** will result in the identification of missing measures or components, and the team can either immediately propose language or identify an accountable **owner** who is responsible for doing the work to determine what a particular measure (or related group of measures) might be and propose language to the team, incorporating it into the **project statement** before the next **definition meeting**.

This team repeats this several times over the course of the **commitment phase**, raising issues in a **definition meeting**, addressing those issues after the meeting, learning and iterating.

Gradually, over the course of the **commitment phase**, the **project statement** evolves from an incomplete, approximate hypothesis about what the project might be to a committed description of what the project is. The actual adjustments and improvements are made both inside **definition meetings** and as results of **action items** individual owners agree to deliver between those meetings.

Pro Tips

Getting Creative in Your Measures of Success

Here is an example of a corporate client that was able to redefine their **customer measures of success** in a way that ultimately changed their business.

> The client is a manufacturer of ice machines. Instead of racing to create the lowest cost machine, they had an interesting piece of technology that made their ice machine small and quiet. Because of this feature, they targeted nurse stations in hospitals and discovered something interesting that was needed by their potential new customer. One of the key attributes and measures of customer success was the "chewability" of the ice by patients.

> Ice chewability presented a dilemma, even for these experts. They knew chewability was a function of some combination of frozen water and liquid water and blended-in air, but they had no idea how to engineer those specifications. And how could it ever be a measurable attribute?

They were faced with an extraordinary problem, and they knew if they could get it right, they would be hugely successful. Should they simply say the ice was supremely chewable and not worry about measuring it? That was risky, because they might be wrong.

They were forced to get creative, and in the face of making the unmeasurable measurable, they created the ICAB—the Ice Chewability Approval Board. The ICAB consisted of the head of sales, the program manager, the product manager, and the CEO. The idea was that when the ICAB gave a thumbs-up, the ice would be deemed chewable. Once the board was created, it went into the project statement, and this allowed them to use it within their product development structure and schedule around it.

Using language and creativity, they solved the problem of measurability for the customer requirement that the ice be chewable. Creating a common language around ice chewability and the structure of the board allowed the engineers to ask the question whether or not their newest iteration would "pass the ICAB." This sentence then led to the actions that were needed to make this happen. Maybe they created early versions. Perhaps they had the ICAB test samples and share what they liked and what they didn't. The point is that before the measure of the ICAB was in place, there was not a way to put specs around this most important criterion.

The story has a happy ending. Using the ICAB, they achieved the chewability of ice that their customer required. They moved out of producing a commodity piece of machinery and now manufacture the most elite ice-machine product on the market.

We insist **customer measures of success** be measurable. If you can't measure it, you can't know whether you are done or not. We push teams to strive for numbers, because it is easier and more reliable to design tests against numeric goals. But the ice chewability example shows that it is not necessary. The crucial thing is to settle on a mechanism for deciding unambiguously whether the capability or characteristic described by the **customer measure of success** in fact exists or not by the end of the project.

If that involves inventing a language game ("Did we pass the ICAB?"), we are all for it.

What to Put In, What to Leave Out

We insist the **project statement** be constrained to three or fewer pages. This length limitation is intended to serve as a productive constraint, forcing the team to identify what they must say in what may be the only document that the entire team and management will all read in its entirety.

If this is the only thing a manager read about your project, would it say what needed to be said?

The key is to carefully consider and craft the language—often adding or modifying a single word will convey a world of useful information. Brief phrases may have extensive research and analysis hidden behind them. For example, the **project end date** may have behind it an entire complex schedule or work breakdown structure that takes all the things that need to be done and all the resources available to do it and organizes all that to finally express a single **project end date**. Only the result appears on the **project statement**. All the work that went into figuring out that result may (or may not) be recorded in other structures, tools, or documents.

It is not right to say that the **project statement** is focused on a particular (or particularly high) "level of detail." Teams will be looking at all levels of project detail to pick out the measures they need to mention because leaving them out would be too risky. You want to err on the side of rigorous **transparency** for items that are controversial or surprising.

Before the **commitment phase** can end, the team must confirm the elements of the **project statement** "hang together." Use this checklist to ensure your project statement is both clear and correct, referring to *the actual words you wrote down*.

♦ Check: The **target customer** is who you intend to target. It is defined to be narrow enough that you can satisfy them and broad (or wealthy) enough they will generate sufficient profit to justify the project.

♦ Check: The **customer measures of success** are both necessary and sufficient to satisfy the **target customer**, such that you will achieve your **business measures of success**. In other words, they will buy what you are building.

♦ Check: The **business measures** include a credible projection of what profit you anticipate by delivering the capabilities described by the given **customer measures of success** to the given **target customer**. They include a credible projection of your costs to build, deploy, and deliver those capabilities. You are satisfied that this profit is sufficiently valuable, that the project is worth doing given this cost. The organization is committed to tracking the **business measures** over the period that these profits and costs are accruing.

♦ Check: The **components**, as given, are both necessary and sufficient to unlock every capability included in the **customer measures of success** as given.

All these checks represent various properties of a well-formed **project statement** that demonstrate it is self-consistent, it "hangs together." If any of these properties are broken or missing from the **project statement**, the **commitment phase** continues, and the team must get into action to fix these issues prior to the next **definition meeting**.

Testing

It is important to recognize you must have a testing and quality assurance process on your team with an accountable **owner**. That owner is on the hook to ensure your **customer measures of success** are demonstrably achieved by the end of your project. This is one of the reasons why it is so critical to have the quality assurance representatives in the room during **definition meetings**. Not only do they need to confirm a **measure of success** is clear and appropriate, but they also need to confirm it is *testable*. It is necessary for projects to allocate resources early to develop and assess the test methodology itself and to invest in whatever test tools and fixtures are required.

Determining Scope

Determining the scope of the project at the highest level is one of the most critical (and complicated) questions teams must answer. It is important to get this clear early in the **commitment phase**. Here are some "best practices" to think about.

Remember, a project is anything with a "a beginning, an end, and a measurable goal." It is important to define when a given project will end. One of the key benefits of dividing your work into explicit projects is this construct can be both flexible and clear. In a commercial setting, a project should encompass all the things necessary to achieve a revenue-producing event. "Time to profit" is the best way to think about a project schedule. A product development project should include all the activities and associated resources necessary to get to that revenue event. In addition to developing the device, it may also include opening a factory, training a salesforce, or developing marketing materials.

The point is to avoid projects that get you only part of the way to profit. For example, if, before you can decide what to build, you need to create a "proof of concept," then we would advise delivering that proof of concept as an (early) milestone of a commercial project, not a project on its own. Such a proof of concept does not, on its own, have a commercial value.

Sometimes a project will include the development of multiple related products, occasionally with different ship dates—this makes sense, for example, if they are all required to achieve a commercial result. We have seen this, for example, in software projects that include both a server product and a client application. If these products all involve the same resources, then it is useful to include them within the same project. This project may have multiple ship dates, one for each product. The project does not end until the last product in the set ships.

Our baseline focuses on usefulness and workability. Give some thought as to what the best use of the overarching project structure is, as it relates to getting to the point of profit. This is one of the most important conversations the empowered and accountable team should wrestle with early in the **commitment phase**.

THE RUF TEAM LIST, WITH INDIVIDUAL ACCOUNTABILITIES DOCUMENTS

Most project managers write and share team lists. Yet, we run into few organizations that have a clear, common understanding of what it means to be "on the team." As a result, their team lists don't say anything specific and clear, and we find individuals are often confused (whether their name is on a list or not) as to whether they are actually "on the team" or not.

In the language of RUF, "on the team" means something specific. If you are accountable for any deliverable the project requires to be successful, *you are on the team.*

The RUF **team list**, then, includes exactly those names of people who have accountabilities on the project. We insist teams maintain their team lists and their associated **individual accountabilities** with **transparency** and **integrity**. That means if someone sees her name on the team list, she knows the team is counting on her to deliver. If an individual is on the hook to deliver a required result, but her name is not on the team list, that team list is broken—it is out of integrity.

For each member of the **project team**, the team list indicates whether that person is on the **core team** or the **extended team**. It also indicates which **track** they belong to, and whether they are the **track leader**.

Maintaining the **integrity** of the **team list** (as with all RUF **project documents**) is the responsibility of the **project leader**.

Prior to the first **definition meeting**, the **project leader** will take her best guess at who will be on the project team. Often, the initial team list is obvious. However, the initial team list is probably wrong. You just don't know in what way it needs to change. Revising the team list is one of the most important concurrent and iterative activities of the commitment phase. Changes in the measures of success, scheduling, and risks may all require changes in the composition of the team. Your objective is to identify and address these changes early in the project.

The **team list** is a simple document. It is a list of the names of team members grouped by track, with their contact information, role, followed by (at most) one document per team member describing her accountabilities on this project.

Here's an example on the next page.

Drafting Individual Accountabilities

There is a specific process RUF invokes for generating the **individual accountabilities** document for each new team member. Suppose you are the new team member:

1. Now that you are on the team, your first step should be to begin drafting your **individual accountabilities**. You

	B	C	D	E	F
1	Team List		Current as of	4/25/2018	
2					
3	Team Member	Role	Location	Email	Phone
4	Katja Rogowski	Project Leader	Bldg 4	k.rog@acme.com	4-1738
5	Arnold Yu	Admin	Bldg 4	a.yu@acme.com	4-2151
6	Ichiko Hashimoto	Lead Architect	Bldg 4	i.hash@acme.com	4-8314
7	Benoit Duplessy	Engineering	Bldg 4	b.dup@acme.com	4-5782
8	Harley Smith	Engineering/Materials	Bldg 4	h.smi@acme.com	4-9131
9	Jane Hashimoto	Product Manager	Bldg 1	j.has@acme.com	1-9241
10	Paul Houston	Market earch		om	1-2046
11	Tina Vo	Sale son			1-1762
12	Ed Simpson	ort Lias		m	1-5242
13	Pramila A upal	as		.com	4-3378
14	Beatric ein	ger	Bldg 1	b.ste@acme.com	1-1021
15					

KEEP IT SIMPLE, BUT KEEP IT IN *INTEGRITY* THROUGHOUT THE PROJECT.

WWW.RISKUPFRONT.COM

Fig. 25: The RUF team list.

may not know anything about the project. In that case, you should talk to the project leader to find out about the project—she may give you a copy of the project statement if there is a draft already developed. You can also speak to your manager or other members of the project team for insight about the project.

2. Don't have someone else write your accountabilities for you. Write down a list of what you understand to be your accountabilities to the project. Depending on circumstances, the entries on the list may be general (e.g., "I am accountable for resolving all issues regarding the database design and implementation," "I am accountable for testing the software") or specific (e.g., The author of module Y might be on the team, saying, "I will be accountable for making sure the feed produced by module X is usable by module Y").

3. The team member schedules and owns a meeting attended by herself, the **project leader**, and her manager (when the manager is someone other than the project leader). They sit down in front of the **individual accountabilities** page she drafted, make any mutually agreeable adjustments, and ultimately agree it is complete and correct. At that point, there is a decision to allocate this individual to this project, with sufficient availability to deliver on the agreed-upon accountabilities.

4. The **project leader** collects those accountabilities, one document for each project team member, into a folder in the shared repository.

Your review meeting is important and has four objectives:

1. You, your functional manager, and the project leader must agree on your accountabilities for this project. We want to make sure you don't find yourself saying yes to demands from the project leader and from your functional manager that conflict. Let's get everyone on the same page early.

2. The review will surface gaps and overlaps in accountabilities among project team members.

3. Out of the review, the functional manager will often identify training, development, coaching, or additional support that she may need to provide you for you to fulfill your accountabilities.

4. The individual accountability review is a powerful DKDK meeting, just like the definition meeting. In both cases, a line-by-line read-through of a document, with all the

right people in the room, uncovers important issues and hidden risks. For example, a recent review of a test engineer's accountabilities at one of our clients highlighted that his previous projects, despite planning, lacked sufficient prototype units for reliability testing. The project leader took several action items to make sure that didn't happen on her project.

Here's an example of an individual accountabilities document for one team member:

Project Olaf
Individual Accountabilities (IAs)

Team Member: Jane Hashimoto

Status: Final, signed off January 19, 2018

Role on Project: Product manager

For this project, you can count on me for:

1. Getting customer information, including:

    a. Customer's process qualification plan

    b. Timeline and milestones from customer project and product release road map

    c. Any customer feedback required

2. Business outlook, forecast of adoption and production ramp, cost of being late

3. Negotiation of commercial and technical terms

4. Target customer's definition

5. Approval of use cases for test plans, and Device Compatibility Matrix

---

6. Alignment of "look and feel" with rest of product line

7. Development, resourcing, and execution of product release plan

8. Assist project leader in getting executive sponsorship for the project

Known risks to my participation:

1. Cause: Product manager is only temporary on the project.

   Effect: We will have to revisit the project statement.

   Impact: Schedule will slip.

2. Cause: I am managing two other projects.

   Effect: It will take longer to complete commitment phase; issues will get missed.

   Impact: Delay in establishing committed end date of project

Three-way review meeting completed and signed off by:

Team Member (taking on IAs):
Jane Hashimoto

Manager (allocating resource to project):
Anil Jayapal

Project Leader (IAs are necessary and sufficient):
Katja Rogowski

Fig. 26: The RUF individual accountabilities document.

By having the new team member take the lead in crafting her own individual accountabilities, she will force herself to get clear on what is being asked of her, and she will think carefully about how she is going to reconcile these new accountabilities with any other responsibilities she has on her plate. It also allows the manager to see where any misunderstandings might crop up. We find this works much better, in practice, than the manager simply telling an employee what to do and presuming the conversation is over.

Pro Tips

The Integrity of the Team List

The **project leader** is accountable for the **integrity** of the **team list**. Because the **team list** includes every individual who is on the hook to deliver something required by the project, only individuals on that list can own risks or **action items**. Remember, the **owner**'s role is causal. Owners certainly might cause (delegate, persuade, cajole, hire, pay) people outside the team to do things that contribute to completing **action items**, but it is the **owner**, the team member, who is on the hook to get it done.

The **integrity** of the **team list** is simple: the list is "in integrity" if the names on the list match the set of people who are accountable to deliver results required by the project.

To avoid breakdowns:

◆ When an action item is being recorded, and the obvious person to own it is not currently on the team (or present in the meeting), don't list them as the **owner**! Get an actual, present team member to agree to own the action item so the team member is now accountable. She is free to handle it as she needs to. She might deliver the result, or she might cause the nonmember to do it, or she might recruit that person onto the team and negotiate with him to accept ownership of the action item.

♦ If a team member leaves the team, make sure she gets taken off the **team list**! Then make sure all her accountabilities, **action items**, and risks are assigned to a new **owner**. If this occurs unexpectedly during the **delivery phase**, it may represent a breakdown—the team was counting on that individual when they committed to the project, and now they are not committed. You may need to adjust the other RUF project definition documents to account for the change. Make sure you reestablish team commitment when that happens.

Accountability Review in Matrix Organizations

In a **matrix organization**, each employee reports to a **functional manager**, who in turn assigns the employee to projects that have (separately) their own **project leaders**. A project leader will be working with teams consisting of participants from various functional groups, and each team member has commitments to both their functional manager and to the project leader.

For the **individual accountabilities document** to have **integrity** in such an organization, it is important to have three people in the review meeting: the individual, the project leader, *and* the functional manager. Each of the three participants is asking a distinct question to decide whether or not to sign off on the document.

- **The individual employee:** Do I commit to being held accountable for these things? Am I able to do them?

- **The functional manager:** Can I allocate this individual to spend the time required by the project to do these things? Are they available to do the work, given all the other demands on our functional group?

- **The project leader:** Are the accountabilities, as written, both necessary and sufficient for what the project requires from this individual? Will these accountabilities, in conjunction with those of the other team members, cover everything the project needs? Is there any overlap or confusion with other team members' accountabilities?

We consider this meeting a critical best practice. It is not sufficient to pass emails and documents back and forth; there must be a meeting.

This meeting will straighten out many of the common breakdowns that occur in matrix organizations when an individual's day-to-day activities are oriented around a project rather than direct assignment by her functional manager.

In this conversation, we want the individual to be clear on what she will be accountable for on this project and agree that this is both appropriate and doable. We also want the **project leader** and the functional manager to both agree that this is what this individual should be doing on this project.

A familiar problem for many team members is they find themselves saying yes to various commitments both to the **project leader** and to their functional manager even when those commitments may be incompatible during the life of the project. We expect teams to identify and resolve issues related to those conflicts at the front end of the project. These resolutions may take various forms such as the following:

- The actual accountabilities can be clarified, refined, or narrowed so the individual and her functional manager agree they are compatible with her other responsibilities, and the **project leader** agrees they meet the needs of the project.

- The functional manager may suggest that another member of her functional group is better suited to take those accountabilities on the project.

- The **project leader**, having heard concerns from the functional manager, may identify a way to split the roles in the project in a different way or may drive the team to change their project tradeoff (e.g., reducing scope) to allow the individual to participate in a way that accommodates her other constraints or commitments.

Notice we are leveraging rigorous **accountability** and **transparency** to uncover risks associated with resource issues. We have found that problems with roles and responsibilities are one of the major sources for failed projects. The functional manager in these reviews may identify that this is not the right person to have those accountabilities.

THE RUF WEEKLY SCHEDULE

To capture the **action items** the team has identified are necessary to achieve a successful project, your team will focus on the RUF **weekly schedule.** It is designed to focus the team on maintaining a high level of **integrity** and **commitment** reliably over the entire duration of the project.

The RUF Approach to Scheduling

Many teams use scheduling tools to break down their work, note dependencies, assign resources, estimate task durations, and come with a "project schedule." Often, the project schedule will be reported in the form of a Gantt chart, PERT chart, or task calendar. In our experience, these tools are useful for figuring out what the elements of work for a project should be and what are reasonable estimates for when things will get done. However, they are terrible for pacing the team and tracking progress. They focus too much on descriptions and not enough on commitments.

Fig. 27: Reframe project schedules into weekly deliverables.

We recommend that teams use these tools, as required, at the beginning of their project to develop the list of what needs to happen and when they expect each result in the list to be done. Group those results by track (engineering, marketing, legal, documentation, testing, and whatever your project requires). Then divide all the identified tasks into weekly buckets, based on their expected completion dates, and enter these deliverables into the **weekly schedule**. To be clear, this does not necessarily mean the work happens in that week (it may span several weeks) but rather the team can count on the **owner** to complete it by the end of that week.

The team can then focus on delivering a successful project by delivering a series of successful project weeks.

The Project Week

We have talked about using the RUF **weekly accountability meeting (WAM)** to create a rhythm on your project, instilling a repeatable and reliable "commit and deliver" behavior on the team that keeps your project on track. The week prior to each **WAM** is its "project week."

The **weekly schedule** is contained in a single spreadsheet document, maintained in your shared project document repository. The document contains one tab (each tab is an individual spreadsheet) for each project week. Each tab is labeled with the date of that week's **WAM**.

Each tab for a project week contains a spreadsheet representing the **weekly deliverables** that have deadlines falling within that project week. Each row of the spreadsheet represents one deliverable.

Weekly Deliverables and Other Action Items

In any meeting or conversation, or even when you are alone thinking about your work, you are writing down **action items**. These items represent things you discover must get done. As you write **action items** down, always explicitly account for the following three parameters:

♦ **Deliverable:** A description in language that is clear, specific, and measurable

♦ **Owner:** The name of the individual who agrees to be accountable for causing that result on time

♦ **Due:** The date by which the result will be delivered

> **Weekly schedule:** The spreadsheet of all your project's weekly deliverables, divided by project week. Transparently shared with the entire team always.
>
> **Weekly deliverable:** An action item for a result or milestone that is tracked by the core team. No track of the project should go more than two weeks without some weekly deliverable.
>
> **Action item:** A written record of a result required on your project, with an identified owner committed to causing that result by an identified deadline.
>
> **WAM:** Weekly accountability meeting. The RUF practice that establishes, tracks, and maintains accountability, transparency, integrity, and commitment throughout your project.
>
> **Project week:** The workweek prior to a WAM. The integrity of all the commitments with deadlines falling within that week are accounted for (done/not done) in that WAM.

If any of these parameters are missing, your action item is out of **integrity**. The action item is also broken if (1) the **owner** is not in fact committed to causing the result by the stated deadline, or (2) the description of the result is ambiguous or unmeasurable, such that the team won't be able to tell if it is done or not. Don't let this happen.

Some items represent low-level task outcomes; others represent major results or consolidated milestones. The **action items** that rise to the level of tracking by the team at the **WAM** are considered **weekly deliverables**, and those **action items** are recorded on the appropriate tabs of the **weekly schedule**.

Fig. 28: The RUF weekly schedule.

Task Dependencies

What about task dependencies? Experienced project managers, who are used to tracking projects with complex task dependency management or sophisticated resource allocation tools, may be skeptical that a project can be managed with such simple lists. The reason this is possible is based on our focus on **integrity** and **commitment** of accountable action item owners.

Some project management methods and tools (we're looking at you, Microsoft Project) assign people to tasks as if they were (more or less) interchangeable finite blocks of labor applied to activity. When you use those methods naively, you will find yourself assigning people to tasks by clicking on a computer screen and then finding yourself caring a lot about how you will have to change your scheduled tasks when some activity is delayed, and dependent activities must be adjusted. In fact, a common breakdown in schedules created by dependency management software is to inadvertently leave out a dependency that was in the team's blind spot. It is only discovered at the worst possible moment, when an activity is scheduled to begin, and the assigned team member informs the project manager she cannot begin because of some unforeseen missing input. And the entire team will say to one another, "It just happens. Oh well."

But on a RUF project, activities are not assigned by a project manager; they are owned by an accountable team member, who is committed (even in the face of circumstances such as dependencies that might be late) that the activity results will be delivered by a deadline. Suddenly, it is the *accountable team member's responsibility* to understand her dependencies and ensure they come in on time. She must make sure those dependencies have owners who are committed to their timely delivery, and the risks associated with those dependencies are identified and mitigated. She has to do this in order to robustly commit to the team that she will deliver on time. In fact, she is often much better positioned to accurately understand what her dependencies are and what she needs to do to effectively mitigate the risk that they may be late. A project manager, who is trying to account for dependencies in every area of the project (especially on large, complex projects), working with a team that is not obsessively focused on identifying and mitigating risk is likely to miss those dependencies.

If team members are clear on this shift in context and accountability, all your other tools for managing dependencies, such as Gantt charts, can certainly be brought to bear.

Instead of using a system that makes it technically easy to reschedule in the face of expensive slips, we replace it with a system that makes expensive slips less likely to occur because we proactively consider the risks that slips might happen, and we engage the team in mitigating those risks in order to make their **commitment** robust.

There is an additional benefit to focusing the team on results and **accountability** rather than the usual tasks and assignments. By allowing the team to demonstrate they have what it takes to deliver on their commitments week after week, the **project leader** is no longer stuck micromanaging all the concurrent things that are going on. The 100 percent **weekly percent complete** provides concrete evidence that the team has their deliverables under control. Further, team members who are accountable owners need not be told, step by step, what to do; rather, they will thoughtfully negotiate what is the required outcome. When they need advice or assistance on how to get something done, they are expected to ask for it. Team members are free to, and expected to, leverage their skill, experience, creativity, and ability to negotiate and escalate to get what they need to be successful.

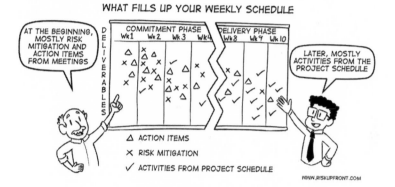

Fig. 29: What fills up your weekly schedule.

How It Gets Written

Weekly deliverables arrive onto the **weekly schedule** from a variety of sources, as shown in the above "deliverables funnel."

- **From scheduling activity.** As described above, the initial project scheduling activity will result in estimated dates for results, deliverables, and milestones associated with each of the **tracks** of the project, and those will get entered into the **weekly schedule.**

- **From new team members as they join.** As the **project leader** is initially recruiting project team members onto the project, they may agree there are things the new project member should take on immediately, even prior to the first **definition meeting**. The two of them craft those things into **action items**, and they go onto the **weekly schedule**. The first action item for a new member is usually, "Complete RUF checklist to draft your **individual accountabilities**, deliver reviewed list to **project leader** for inclusion on **team list**."

♦ **From risks.** Team members are obligated to surface risks as they identify them, and although there are practices where the team is specifically focused on identifying risks collaboratively, individuals might identify risks at any time. As each risk is recorded, it is taken by an **owner**. In deciding what needs to be done to mitigate that risk, she will craft **action items** (negotiating their owners and deadlines) that she will feed to the **weekly schedule**.

♦ **From any meeting.** At DKDK meetings of the entire **core team**, the scratchpad action item list is readily available, and whenever the team realizes that something needs to get done, they can craft language to add the action item then and there. From smaller problem-solving meetings, the meeting **owner** can collect the resulting **action items** and send them to the **weekly schedule**.

♦ **From a definition meeting.** As the team records language on the **project statement** that contains a tentative or hypothetical claim, the team should record an action item to put someone on the hook to nail it.

♦ **From a WAM. Action items** will be identified in deciding how to respond to items that are "not done" in reviewing and refining commitments for the upcoming week and adjusting the schedule and out of the "top two risks" conversation.

♦ **From other action items.** Finally, the team will record **action items** that specifically result in other lists of **action items**.

This last case, **action items** to create **action items**, may seem strange, but it is common and useful. For example, suppose you know you need a meeting to solve a problem. However, you are not exactly sure who should be in the meeting, perhaps because you're not sure who knows the most about your problem, or you're not sure who is on vacation. So because you can't now commit to a deadline to solve the problem, you commit to an interim deadline to agree on a deadline. That may take some effort.

> **Katya:** OK, so we need to agree on the database schema. Irfan, can you finish that by February 1?
>
> **Irfan:** Wait a second, Belinda and I are figuring out what database platform to use, and the schema depends on that.
>
> **Katya:** Good catch. By when will you be able to figure that out?
>
> **Irfan:** Belinda, can we meet on Monday with the database team to settle that date?
>
> **Belinda:** Yes, in the morning.
>
> **Katya:** Action item: "Meeting with Belinda and database team. *Owner*: Irfan. Deadline: Monday." What do we think is your *measure of success* for that meeting?

> **Irfan:** It will be to agree on a committed date for delivery of the database schema.
>
> **Katya:** OK, after the meeting, let me know your committed date for when I'll see the schema in the document repository.
>
> **Irfan:** Will do!

When you can't give the **project leader** a committed date for an important result, give her the date *by which you'll know* that committed date. Sometimes you don't even know, in the moment, when the right people will be able to meet—so then you commit to finding a time and getting the meeting scheduled on your teammates' calendars. Congratulations. You've just committed to the scheduling deadline, which will determine the meeting deadline, which will determine the agreement deadline. The point is, there is always some next step you can commit to that represents concrete progress toward your goal.

Pro Tips

Urgency on All Tracks

There is a temptation to allow certain areas of the project to go several weeks without having any deliverables tracked in the **WAM**. For example, if the legal team is going off and drafting contracts, perhaps they won't have a result for a month. Or it will take six weeks to build a required software library.

We train teams to make sure every **track** produces some valuable result at the **WAM**, if not every week, then at least every two weeks. For example, if you tell me you require six weeks to build a software library, I would ask you, "What must be true at the end of two weeks, without which you'd probably fail to deliver at week six?" You might say, "At the end of week two, the library spec document will be reviewed and approved. At the end of week four, twelve of the fifteen functions will be written. At the end of week six, all functions will be committed and unit tests will have been written, run, and passed." These deliverables can then be entered into the **weekly schedule** for the Software track.

Note even **tracks** that seem to have deliverables only at the end of the process (perhaps testing or operational activity) can get into action early on the project, focusing on mitigating risks.

Clear Language Now, No Arguments Later

Watch out for results language that is not specific and measurable. You want to assess and upgrade your language at the moment when it is written down. Ask yourself, "Will there be a disagreement later, within the team, as to whether the results were actually achieved or not?" You wish that, as the **owner** of an action item, you were the arbiter of whether it is done or not. Unfortunately, other team members are reading your action item and making their own decisions and commitments based on what they think you are committed to, based on what you've written.

Consider this first attempt at crafting the language for an action item:

> Complete individual accountabilities.
> Owner: Pramila. Deadline: June 5, 2015

We want you (the **owner**, the **project leader**, anyone who sees this projected in front of a meeting) to raise obvious questions: What does "complete" mean? Do I just need to write my accountabilities down? How many? If I write them down but haven't yet sent it to the **project leader**, is this action item done or not done? (It could go either way—maybe you expect to have another action item to send your **individual accountabilities** to the **project leader**.) The point is, it is toxic to leave those words, as they stand, on a page shared with the team. Answer those questions. When your team is good at this, you will probably end up with something like this:

> Schedule review of my draft of my individual
> accountabilities, deliver reviewed list to
> project leader. Owner: Pramila. Deadline:
> June 5, 2015

This, in a few words, encapsulates all the valuable aspects of creating **individual accountabilities**: that they are drafted by the individual, that they are reviewed in a meeting, and that they end up in the **project leader**'s hands for inclusion in the **team list** and **individual accountabilities** document.

Focus Action Items on Valuable End Points
It is common to create separate **action items** for the "steps" to get to a result. Don't do that. Instead of recording an **action item** for the task, then another for the communication of the result, then another for getting it reviewed, and

so forth, simply articulate the valuable end point in a single action item with a single owner. Using careful language, you can set your expectations precisely. For example, by saying, "Deliver reviewed list to **project leader**," you are making it clear what the project needs is not just your list but your list at a certain level of quality ("reviewed") in the hands of the person who needs it ("to **project leader**"). Trust the **owner** to handle the steps outside of the **weekly schedule** if the risks are low enough to allow her to robustly commit.

When You Need Commitment

During the **commitment phase** of the project, the team has not yet committed to overall project results—they haven't yet agreed on what the project is. But we have said repeatedly that an action item, written into the **weekly schedule**, represents an **owner** committed to deliver a thing. Let's give that a bit of nuance.

At each **WAM**, when reviewing the commitments due in the coming week, owners must affirm that those commitments are robust. They will be so.

For **action items** due in future weeks that are recorded during the **commitment phase**, the team must understand they don't yet know all the risks they have, or what the project even is, and so the results and deadlines may not be reliable. Actions that the team thought were necessary may become unnecessary as the **project definition** evolves and vice versa. So as you record an action item, you should still take its deadline seriously, identify risks that stand in your way, submit those risks, and record additional **action items** to mitigate them. Those "mitigation" action items have their own committed owners. Project leaders, when they have one-on-one conversations with team members, can productively ask, "Are *any* of your upcoming commitments at risk of not being done on time?" This provides a way to prompt team members to get into action on their risks and improve their ability to deliver their week-by-week commitments.

During the **delivery phase**, every **commitment** on the **weekly schedule** must remain robust. Don't commit to results and dates that the project doesn't need you to commit to. Where a **commitment** is necessary, get the risks to successful delivery under control before you record your **commitment**. That may entail you or other team members agreeing to be accountable for **action items** that cause urgent risk mitigation.

THE RUF RISK ACTION PLAN

At the core of Risk Up Front is a "language game" that changes how your team talks about risk. In chapter 5, we walked through the details of **cause**, **effect**, **impact**, how changing the team's language changes behavior, and how changes in behavior lead to changes in results. We expect teams to be using this way of talking about risk in every project conversation, all over the project.

We have designed the **risk action plan** for recording, prioritizing, and tracking risk identification and mitigation so that it leverages this new way of talking about risk.

But let's step back a moment and see how so-called risk lists go wrong.

> As the project schedule is being made, the project manager collects a list of risks on the project.
>
> She walks around her team, asking what people are worried about. She hears things like, "Our vendor is so disorganized; they'll probably deliver the test chip late," or "You want us to change the database schema? We won't be able to update all the database servers without impacting existing clients."
>
> The manager diligently writes these risks down in a list. Perhaps she holds some meetings, and people promise to watch these things closely. The list ends up in a drawer, having made no impact on the project plan.
>
> Then, when the project has run into a ditch, she pulls the risk list out, shows it to management, saying, "See? We knew it might fail for this very reason."

That thing you called a risk list was an excuse list. Because most teams naturally view risks as *bad news*, it makes sense they'd want to sweep them into a drawer and get on with their work.

But teams trained to use RUF view risks as *good news*, because they lead to valuable action. Identifying and mitigating a risk is like dodging a bullet. What would a tool look like that caused a team to mitigate their risks reliably?

The RUF **risk action plan**, which our clients have taken to calling their "**RAP sheet**," is designed to impose **accountability**, **transparency**, **integrity**, and **commitment** onto the identification and mitigation of risk. For it to accomplish this, the

project leader is accountable for ensuring that *every* team member is engaged in identifying project risks from the beginning. The **RAP sheet** does not sit in a drawer or remain hidden on a server. It is a living document that is reviewed and managed no less than weekly by the team.

One of our early clients remarked, "The team spends less time complaining in the break room." By having a **RAP sheet** in the face of your project team, you will notice that when a team member is complaining of some worry or concern, other team members will respond, "Great! Have you submitted a RAP?" By formulating their concern and having the **project leader** record it, complaint will be turned into action.

The RAP Sheet Format

The **risk action plan** is a spreadsheet document with two tabs. The first is for **active risks**. As risks are mitigated, they are cut and pasted to the second tab, **closed risks**. You enter each risk on a single row of the spreadsheet, filling out the following columns.

Risk ID

The Risk ID must be a unique identifier. We recommend you use the **track** or category in which this risk falls plus a number. This makes it easy to refer to risks with precision. For example, instead of "the database risk" it is "Database-2." This helps when using tools such as Jira to record risks. Often, a category is the track in which the risk falls. For complex projects, there might be multiple categories (e.g., "database performance"), with their own accountable owners, within a track.

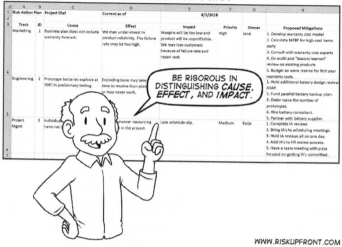

Fig. 30: The RUF risk action plan spreadsheet.

Submitted On, Submitted By

When a risk is added to the **risk action plan**, the submitter and date are noted. This lets the team know how long the risk has been known on the project.

Cause

This is the currently true condition that is causing you to worry about some potential future bad outcome. It must have already occurred.

Effect

The future possible bad outcome that will cause the project to fail. It must not have occurred yet.

Impact

If the effect does come to pass, what impact will this have on the project? What will fail? What **measure of success** or **business measure** is in jeopardy?

Priority

The RUF risk prioritization scheme is a four-point scale (1: Super-high risk, 4: Low risk), discussed in detail below.

Owner

Who (by name) on the team is accountable for mitigating this risk? Typically, it's the person who knows the most about it. The **project leader** gets this person's agreement to own the risk before writing her name into the **risk action plan** as the **owner**.

Mitigations

These are proposed mitigations. The **owner** has the final say on which ones will be executed, by creating **action items** in the **weekly schedule**. Any one idea in this field need not fully mitigate the risk; it may, for example, help clarify what the impact of the risk is or narrow the effect of the risk. Teams often get stuck here naming only one or two mitigation ideas. It takes practice for teams to realize they can come up with many mitigation ideas quickly for any risk. We insist the submitter of a risk come up with no less than five. Thereafter, the **owner** can add more, initiate a meeting to add or refine, and eventually decide on what mitigation activity will be done.

Notes

The **submitter**, **owner**, or **project leader** can add additional information about the risk in this field.

How It Gets Written

Submitting Risks

As we said in part 1, the process for identifying risks must be as easy and frictionless as possible, and the bar for submitting risks must be kept low. A risk is "identified" when it is submitted for inclusion in the **risk action plan**. On small projects, that may mean sending an email to the project leader. On larger projects, teams may have administrative support and tools (such as Atlassian) to manage and track submissions.

Whenever a team member has identified a risk, she will submit it for inclusion in the **risk action plan**. She must provide the **project leader** with at least the following information:

◆ Carefully crafted language for the **cause, effect**, and **impact** of the risk

◆ An estimated **priority** of the risk

◆ A suggested **owner**

◆ Five proposed mitigations (Really, five. Get creative.)

The **project leader** will ensure that this is entered into the **risk action plan** with a **Risk ID** and committed **owner**. The **owner** must agree to own the risk, so if she has not already done so, the **project leader** must get the **owner**'s consent before finalizing the **owner** field.

When a risk has been mitigated to the extent that it does not stand in the way of the team's **commitment** to successfully completing the project, it can then be cut and pasted from the **active** tab to the **closed** tab. This is based on agreement among the **project leader**, risk submitter, and risk owner. If another team member believes there is still an unmitigated risk to the project, then she can resubmit it. She may feel some important aspect of the closed risk was overlooked and can point that out in her submission.

The ability of any team member to resubmit a risk is an important safety net for keeping the team aware of blind spots.

Prioritizing Risk

Teams are tempted to use sophisticated probability and impact models to prioritize their risks. We find this almost always unhelpful. When prioritizing a risk, the team's familiarity and previous experience with the risk is the single most important factor to consider when deciding how to apply resources for mitigation.

If your team is unfamiliar with the risk, then their assessment of the danger will be unreliable and probably too optimistic. The ways in which it can doom your project are hidden in your team's blind spots.

In recognizing this, RUF proposes a simple four-point scale for prioritizing risks for action:

1. **Super-high:** No one anywhere has ever successfully mitigated this risk before.

2. **High:** Our team has never successfully mitigated this risk before.

3. **Medium:** We've encountered and successfully mitigated this risk but not always.

4. **Low:** We regularly encounter and mitigate this risk.

Assign the priority of a risk using this four-point scale, focusing just on the familiarity of your team with the risk. Then, if you think its impact is particularly severe, you may bump its priority up one level.

Pro Tips

Generalized Worries and Complaints

We have emphasized repeatedly the importance of asking for and offering robust **commitment** to deliver results and not allow the team to devolve into "We'll try our best." As you begin to upgrade your **commitment**, you will notice that you become more hesitant to commit. This is as it should be.

Be on the lookout for things that sound like "worries" or "complaints." Don't dismiss them; rather, use them as an opening to find out what the real cause, effect, and impact are that stand in the way of your **commitment**. Work together with your teammates to refine your worry into an actionable risk and get it on the **risk action plan**.

Specificity of the Cause

Remember the example we used earlier in the book:

> Suppose I say to you, "I'm worried that I'll get into a car accident on my way home from work." What might you say to me in response?

"I'm so sorry to hear that," or "Well, I certainly hope not," or "Drive carefully!"

Now, suppose I say to you instead, "I just noticed the tread on my car tires has worn all the way down, so I'm worried that I'll get into a car accident on my way home from work." What might you say to me in response now? "Let's call my garage. They can send out a truck that will replace your car tires right here in the parking lot."

The more specific the **cause**, the more actionable the risk. If you hear a teammate raise a risk with a cause such as, "We don't have enough resources," consider asking, "Where specifically are you worried we are shorthanded? Are we missing a legal resource? A Python developer? Is the team noticing that a needed skill is not available, or a particular result will need more time given the available resources?"

Often, you will notice as you get more specific that a risk gets rewritten as multiple risks. For example, the general worry about insufficient resources may raise a host of specific risks, such as the following:

[Cause] We don't have any database developer on board, [effect] so we don't know when the database implementation will be completed; [impact] we can't commit to a project end date.

[Cause] Nobody on the team has JavaScript experience...

[Cause] Last time, the team took three weeks to do this, but we're allowing only two weeks in the schedule, and one person has left the team...

All these examples are more specific than "We don't have enough resources," and each suggests its own world of opportunities for mitigation.

As we say, "Rows in Excel are cheap; you can make more." Don't try to make the **risk action plan** entries high level and few. Make them detailed and many. Set your priorities and get creative about mitigation.

Make it very easy for your team to submit entries onto the risk list, then use the RUF priorities to determine the allocation of scarce mitigation resources.

Creativity in the Mitigations

From the early days of jet airplanes, it has been known that bird strikes against jet engines carried the risk of catastrophic engine failure. Since the early 1950s, aircraft manufacturers have tested their engines to ensure they would withstand bird strikes. They would shoot a variety of materials, including various clays, gelatins, and even ground meat, at high speed into running jet engines to see what might cause catastrophic failure. Ultimately, they determined that only real birds would do. They developed a "chicken gun" that would shoot whole chickens (not live ones!) at engines running full speed in a specially designed wind tunnel to mimic the effects of a bird strike. These tests were done while the engine was being developed (early!) and again when undergoing final certification. Of course, testing the engine while it is in the air with passengers, when a real bird strike would occur, would be far too late.

Look for ways to "chicken test" risky components of your project. It must happen long before the final deliverables are completed, so you will have to invent a test that simulates the real-world effect of the risk on the component, perhaps on a prototype, perhaps in a test environment. Do this *unusually* early in the project schedule to test a key assumption or confirm a performance level. Teams require creativity and flexibility to come up with useful chicken tests. We love to hear risk owners say, "We should chicken-test that!"

In our workshops, we do several exercises to show teams what it is like to invent mitigations for risks. As soon as they get the cause down to a specific case, some mitigations come easily. "Nobody on the team has JavaScript experience," quickly leads to, "Hervé, we're sending you off to JavaScript camp," or "João, you are going to JSCon to recruit a JavaScript programmer." Teams find it easy to get one or two ideas.

But it is extremely powerful for teams to stretch outside their comfort zone in developing mitigation ideas. You should be open to ideas that seem outlandish, because they can be a stepping stone to more ideas that fall in the realm of the possible. For example, we have seen a team member suggest mitigating a risk by piping up with, "We could buy company X!" Everyone laughs, and then the person sitting next to her says, "Well, you know, we actually could partner with company X." Suddenly, people stop laughing.

A mitigation idea need not necessarily make the risk disappear, but it may simply make progress. It might change the risk from a high priority to a lower priority (by increasing our familiarity with what is going on), or it may be a proposal that allows the team to learn more about it to enable subsequent, more powerful mitigations.

We routinely see teams that are overloaded with the day-to-day build work of their projects. Make sure your teams have time to generate, explore, and execute creative mitigations. Project teams that fail to innovate, because members are too busy and do not have time for exploratory activities, cannot mitigate their risks. It is critical to explicitly require time blocks early in the project schedule for the brainstorming of creative risk mitigations. Without it, teams will do their day-to-day work and never effectively mitigate their risks.

Also, when you are thinking about mitigating risks (adjusting the "Why Not" of the **5W tradeoff**), make sure you consider all the other axes as possible trades. For example:

- **Who:** Might we add or reassign a team member to mitigate this risk?

- **What:** Might we mitigate this risk by changing what we're building or by dropping a feature?

- **When:** Would it be less risky if we gave ourselves more time?

- **Why:** If we adjust whom we consider to be our **target customer**, might that mitigate the risk? For example, we may discover that by focusing our project on satisfying customer A instead of customer B, we might choose a feature set that is less risky to deliver. Perhaps an alternate **target customer** is less sensitive to a **measure of success** that happens to be risky for us to deliver successfully.

When you submit a risk to the **risk action plan**, always suggest *five mitigations*. The team can come up with even more, and ultimately the **owner** will decide what the appropriate mitigation strategy should be. Both the risk and updated mitigation plan must be shared transparently, so the team can support and perhaps improve the effort.

This is a place where teams need to invest in "exploration" before "exploitation." Rigor helps to create a culture of innovation and creativity. What is rigor in this case? It means insisting on at least five proposed mitigations for every submitted risk. At first, teams may find this a stretch, but quickly, it will become second nature.

Contingency and Backup Plans

When you are looking for ways to mitigate your highest risks, explicitly consider contingency and backup plans.

A **contingency plan** is a road map for what you will do if, and only if, a risk materializes. The process of developing a contingency plan will let the team identify what needs to happen if a disaster strikes. Also, importantly, the team will clarify what the impact on the project will be. For example, the time and resource cost to execute the contingency plan could represent the specific impact of the risk on your project schedule and budget.

It is common to develop contingency plans during the **commitment phase**. If the contingency plan, as designed, persuades the team that the resulting impact is acceptable, you may downgrade the risk.

A **backup plan** involves intentionally resourcing duplicate work. For example, suppose your project depends on a vendor to deliver a prototype of a very complex power supply, one that has never been built before—that would be a super-high risk. You might decide to hire *two* vendors to each build and deliver the component. If the first one delivers successfully, you won't use the second one. The cost to build the backup component is not wasted money; it is *insurance* to protect you from the high cost of a potential vendor failure. You're making a tradeoff. Instead of spending money to buy features or pull in your schedule, you are spending money to reduce your risk. This makes sense when your **cost of being late** is much higher than the cost of your backup plan.

A contingency plan is one where you decide you will fund plan B if plan A fails. A backup plan is one where you decide you will fund *both* plan A and plan B in parallel. It is possible they both may succeed, in which case you will find yourself discarding one of the otherwise acceptable deliverables.

Trading Off Super-High Risks

As you sort your risk list by priority, notice how many super-high risks you have. If you have more than a few, you should be very suspicious of your team's ability to robustly commit to deliver that project successfully. During the **commitment phase**, explore how you can adjust your project definition by reconsidering your target customer, eliminating customer measures of success, or creatively adding resources in ways that take such risks off the project.

THINGS TO REMEMBER

◆ The key to RUF is a small number of project documents, written and maintained with rigor. They serve as a "forcing function" to change teams' behavior. The paperwork is the booby prize. Engaging the team in developing and clarifying those documents is what leads them to settle issues and make changes early. It is the action that matters.

◆ The **project statement** anchors every **definition meeting**. The **weekly schedule** anchors every **weekly accountability meeting**. These documents must not sit in a drawer.

◆ Let individual team members take the lead in writing their **individual accountabilities**, then negotiate to fill in any gaps or conflicts.

◆ Establish that it is every team member's job to identify and communicate risks.

◆ Focus on prioritizing your risk mitigation activity based on how familiar the team is with each risk, rather than their expected severity.

CHAPTER 9

OTHER USEFUL PRACTICES

REVIEWING AN ACCOUNTABILITY MATRIX

One of the responsibilities of the team is to ensure none of the activities on the project are hanging without any accountable **owner** and that they understand who is expected to be involved in the various big deliverables the project needs to achieve.

By building and sharing an **accountability** matrix, the team can see at a glance who is doing what. It also gives the team a chance to detect breakdowns or inconsistencies between what needs to happen and what team members have signed up for.

The **accountability** matrix is a different "slice" on **accountability**. While the **team list** organizes accountabilities by individual, the **accountability** matrix presents the overall relationship between key project deliverables and team members, clarifying who owns and who is involved in each key deliverable.

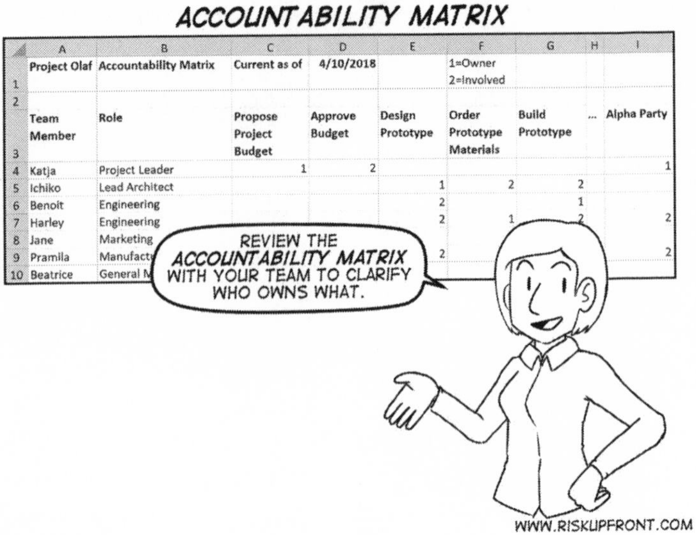

ACCOUNTABILITY MATRIX

	A	B	C	D	E	F	G	H	I
1	Project Olaf	Accountability Matrix	Current as of	4/10/2018		1=Owner 2=Involved			
2									
3	Team Member	Role	Propose Project Budget	Approve Budget	Design Prototype	Order Prototype Materials	Build Prototype	...	Alpha Party
4	Katja	Project Leader	1	2					1
5	Ichiko	Lead Architect			1	2	2		
6	Benoit	Engineering			2		1		
7	Harley	Engineering			2	1	2		2
8	Jane	Marketing							
9	Pramila	Manufactu			2				2
10	Beatrice	General M							

REVIEW THE ACCOUNTABILITY MATRIX WITH YOUR TEAM TO CLARIFY WHO OWNS WHAT.

WWW.RISKUPFRONT.COM

Fig. 31: The RUF accountability matrix spreadsheet.

It is in the form of a matrix; it goes on a single spreadsheet. The columns of the **accountability** matrix contain all the key decisions and milestones of the project, covering all **tracks**. The rows of the project are the members of the project team.

Then in each cell of the matrix, you enter a "1" if that person owns that decision or milestone. Enter a "2" if that person should be involved in that decision or milestone. If neither, the cell is blank.

The key thing to notice is that every column has exactly one "1" in it and any number of "2s." That means every decision and milestone has exactly one **owner**, and the team can see who will be working with the **owner** to achieve the given result.

When you display this in front of the team—for example,

during a **definition meeting**—people will have the chance to notice that some results are unowned or that someone should be involved in a decision, but the **owner** didn't realize it. You can also look at the number of 1s and 2s next to your name and notice perhaps that you are overcommitted on the project and should take your name off a few items.

MANAGING THE PROJECT PORTFOLIO

The RUF Opportunity Sheet

Many organizations need to have a way to feed their pipeline of projects in a rational way. For teams that don't have a system in place, we recommend a simple folder of "opportunity sheets" that systematically describe each opportunity that might turn into a project.

Project Opportunity
Date: 7/25/2016

Submitter: Benoit@sales.newco.com

Opportunity: Sell plugin upgrades to base system to interoperate with database system X.

Target Customer: Acme Widgets and similar

Notes: Acme, along with at least three more of our largest clients, will be moving to system X in the next six months. This will be an easy upsell.

Fig. 32: The RUF opportunity sheet.

The opportunity sheet contains a rough description of the business opportunity and **target customer** for a potential project, along with the submitter name and date submitted. Think of it as something you drop in the "suggestion box" of your organization.

It may also contain an assessment of how many resources this opportunity should consume, given its value. Because you haven't invested any effort in figuring out what the project is (which won't happen until the project is started), you just give your best estimate. A good way to look at this is to complete the sentence, "I would be surprised if this required less than X resources or more than Y resources," and note those bounds as your reasonable guess.

The folder containing these opportunity sheets is a simple and efficient way for teams to note what they can mix and match to form upcoming projects.

You might use similar tools, such as an Agile backlog (things to do but not committed) or Kanban boards (at the project level), to track what the organization is contemplating, what they are committed to defining (whether the **definition phase** has started or not), what is in the process of being defined, what is in the process of being delivered, and what is done. These have all proven useful at a higher level alongside RUF practices deployed within individual projects.

The RUF Project Portfolio Spreadsheet

Most organizations, at any moment, are dealing with multiple projects, some in progress and some on the horizon. Perhaps your organization goes through a budgeting process where you identify the projects you expect to do in the upcoming quarter or year. There is a bit of a paradox that you are asked to budget resources for a project before the project has started and before the team knows exactly what it is. When you are budgeting, all you must go on is your best estimate.

We often see confusion on teams about which projects are under consideration, which ones have been approved, and which ones are under way. It is important to make this transparent throughout your organization. The simplest way to do this is to create a **project portfolio spreadsheet** and maintain it with integrity.

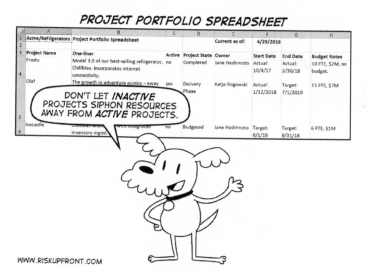

Fig. 33: The RUF project portfolio spreadsheet.

Let's look at the individual columns of the spreadsheet.

Project Name
The name of the project, pulled from the **opportunity sheet** or **project statement**.

Project One-Liner
The one-line description of the project (or a draft of it), from the opportunity sheet or project statement.

Active, Project State
The most important distinction for your project state is *active* versus *inactive*. A project is active if you are expending resources (time, money) on it. The organization must be crystal clear on which projects are active at any point in time. Active projects have a project state indicating what RUF phase they are currently in:

♦ Commitment phase
♦ Delivery phase

Inactive projects can be categorized as the organization deems appropriate, but here is a common set of inactive future project states:

♦ **Proposed:** This is an idea whose merit has not yet been decided.

♦ **Targeted:** We would like to complete this project at a time (often a particular quarter) in the future.

♦ **Budgeted:** We are setting aside resources in anticipation of doing this project. Typically, this refers to scheduled projects for the current budget year.

For projects that have already ended, the project state is as follows:

- **Completed:** The project has met its **measures of success** and ended.

- **Abandoned:** The project has been set aside (for whatever reason), and the team is no longer working on it.

Owner

For active projects, the **owner** is the **project leader.** For inactive future projects, it is the person to whom questions should be addressed. It is often the name of the person you expect to lead the project.

Start Date

For active and ended projects, put the actual start date. For future projects, put a rough idea of when you expect to do it (often simply a year or a quarter, such as 2018Q2 for a project you expect to begin in the second quarter of 2018).

Project End Date

For active and ended projects, this is the **project end date** from the **project statement.** Note that during the **commitment phase,** this is a tentative date, and during the **delivery phase,** this is a committed date. Obviously, for ended projects, it is the date on which the project ended.

Budget Notes

It is often convenient to note, for budgeting, how many resources you are setting aside for this project. In some organizations, this may be FTEs (full-time equivalents, a measure of how many people are involved), or it may be cost estimates.

During the **commitment phase**, as you get a solid idea of how many resources you'll require given the tradeoffs the team is making, you can update this number, which, in turn, may cause you to adjust your other project priorities for the remainder of the budget period. As a matter of fact, the project team can consider these priorities when making its **5W tradeoff** because they will know that the "**cost of being late**" for their project means, concretely, that subsequent projects won't be started as planned.

Pro Tips

Transparency

Make sure the **project portfolio spreadsheet** is always in **integrity** and transparently shared throughout your organization. What does this entail?

- Every project that your organization is working on (or is scheduled to work on) is listed.
- The state of each project is accurately reflected on the list.
- The **accountability** is crystal clear for who decides if a project is going to be resourced.
- Active projects are, in fact, adequately resourced to achieve their stated goal.

We have clients where the management team gathers to review their project portfolio *weekly* to make sure the "above the line" active projects belong there and are being properly resourced.

When the **project portfolio spreadsheet** is in integrity, it serves two functions: it provides an accurate accounting to management of where resources are being deployed, and it indicates unambiguously to employees which projects they should be working on—the active ones.

Overcommitting Your Teams

When managing a project portfolio, the most common problem we see by far is organizations taking on more projects than they have resources to execute successfully.

If you notice your teams are not delivering on their commitments (e.g., as evidenced by their **weekly percent complete** being less than 100 percent), you should first consider that your organization has taken on too much. That's not the only possibility, but it is the most common one.

Critical Resources

It is not enough for a team to have "enough" resources (whatever that means); it must have the right resources. Organizations vary, but we often find, especially in technology organizations, they are constrained by their specialists. These specialists have expertise or experience that is critical to multiple projects.

The key point is, when your specialist is fully allocated to projects, you have reached the limit on the set of projects you can run at one time. Overallocating the time of a required specialist is a common recipe for failed projects.

It is especially critical that functional managers focus regularly on ensuring specialists are delivering successfully on all their commitments across all the projects they are assigned to (this includes participating in the required **DKDK** conversations). If there are slips or breakdowns, it is an indication that the organization is taking on too many projects at once, given the limitations on their access to specialized expertise.

Budgeting Projects

When you go through your project budgeting process, you will assess your best estimate of the value and cost of various opportunities and set your priorities from among your **opportunity sheets**. Sort the project opportunities in your list by priority.

But once you do that—and this is critical—sort the project opportunities by priority, identify the top priorities that fit within your available resources, and draw a line. Make it clear throughout your organization you will not be spending resources on projects below the line.

By the time you share your project list with the team, there is no "priority." There is only "We're planning to do it" and "We're not planning to do it."

Why is this important? Consider this example. Say you are planning out the coming year and reviewing your opportunities to see which ones you will do. Suppose you end up with a list of six potential projects, in priority order, and you estimate you have resources, realistically, to finish the top four this year. In our experience, if you announce your priorities but don't draw a clear line, then this is what will happen: Projects #1 and #2 will get resourced and done, but the team will inadvertently underresource projects #3 and #4, especially in the areas of risk identification and mitigation, while they fritter away resources doing bits and pieces of projects #5 and #6. They'll say, "I don't have anything to do on project #4 at the moment, so I might as well get started on my bit of project #5." Then your team finds itself right back in the land of the "fuzzy front end."

Instead, you want to tear the team away from working on the issues they "know they know" (in this case, scoping out project #5) and instead refocus them on actively identifying and mitigating risks, engaging in deeper **DKDK** conversations and activity, on just those projects that the organization has decided will be done.

THINGS TO REMEMBER

- Use the accountability matrix to clear up confusion and communicate accountabilities particularly in high-risk project areas.

- Use simple but rigorously transparent tools to communicate which projects are active, which are committed, and which are on hold.

- After you prioritize your prospective projects, draw a clear line: projects "above the line" will be resourced, and projects "below the line" will not. Otherwise, your second and third projects will be compromised because you are frittering away resources on lower prioritized projects.

- Kill or stop projects that are not set up for success. Redeploy their resources to get critical projects done faster. Do less sooner!

PART 3

FROM THEORY
TO PRACTICE

In previous chapters, all our examples have been taken from the common threads we see in most projects and teams as they start to apply the structures and practices of Risk Up Front.

In part 3, we are going to consider several specific environments where we have noticed that Risk Up Front brings unexpected benefits. We will also discuss common pitfalls that teams encounter when they apply Risk Up Front and how best to avoid them. It is not our intention to cover the many complex project management issues that these environments present. Rather, we will limit our focus to how the various aspects of these environments impact your use of the Risk Up Front structures and practices.

Specifically, we will discuss the use of Risk Up Front in these types of projects:

- **Industrial Equipment: Big Risk, Big Capital:** These are projects that involve very high capital costs and typically have larger teams, longer schedules, complicated hardware designs, complex supply chains, and more sophisticated controls and governance.

- **Distributed Teams: Spanning Geographies, Time Zones, Languages, and Cultures:** Projects with teams whose participants are geographically separated pose special risks. These often show up in the form of outsourced resources (perhaps developers, manufacturing, operations, testing, or support) that are far away.

- **Startup Companies:** When companies and teams are just coming together, often to build a single product or service and bring it to market for the first time, they may have risks related to doing things that have never been done before.

- **Software Projects and Agile Methodology:** We often work with companies that are using Agile for software development. Agile and RUF work well together. We'll discuss the ways in which RUF can "fill in the holes," given the common ways Agile is deployed.

- **Information Technology: In-House Projects:** Many organizations have in-house projects, both technical and organizational, that develop tools and processes to support the organization, rather than "building something to sell." Many IT department projects fall in this category—for example, "the project to upgrade all the laptops" or "the project to deploy a new internal training system." They also include organizational change projects such as rolling out a new way of doing employee reviews.

- **Organizational Change Projects:** Many of our clients are using Risk Up Front to change the behavior and culture in their organizations. Often after an organizational disruption, such as a reorganization, merger, or layoff, there is an opportunity to mobilize a cross-functional and cross-divisional team to jump-start the organization in the new direction.

- **Not for Profit and Elected Government Offices:** We have applied **Risk Up Front** techniques to projects in government offices, nonprofit organizations, and similar environments. Projects in these environments have much in common with commercial projects, such as the need to control costs and deliver on time. But they vary in how other problems are framed. For example, they often wrestle with questions such as, "Who is the customer?" and "What does **cost of being late** mean when we're not making a profit?"

♦ **Teaching Entrepreneurship: Universities and Incubators:** Finally, we will discuss how we've worked with university entrepreneurship programs and startup incubators to teach the next generation of leaders how to use **Risk Up Front**.

Even if the circumstances of a situation do not seem to apply in your case, we invite you to read through and think about the various optimizations to Risk Up Front practices such teams would make. This will give you greater facility in honing your own team's use of Risk Up Front's language, metrics, practices, and structures.

CHAPTER 10

INDUSTRIAL EQUIPMENT:
BIG RISK, BIG CAPITAL

Our client develops and sells machines other companies use to fabricate integrated circuit "chips." These machines take months to design and develop and cost millions of dollars.

Inside each machine, a slice of silicon wafer is precisely and firmly positioned on an internal mechanism. Various techniques are used to either etch trenches into the wafer or deposit material on the wafer. When complete, the silicon wafer is removed, the next wafer is attached, and the process repeats. These internal components eventually wear out. The etching process takes its toll, and on a regular basis, they need to be replaced. They are complex and expensive.

We were brought onto a project to design one of their chip fabrication machines after they had run into a problem. They had shipped a previous model to one of their customers, who soon noticed these components were wearing out twice as fast as they were told to expect. The customer was refusing to pay for that. Engineers and management got on planes to find out what was causing the problem and smooth over the strained relationship with their customer. Ultimately, the manufacturer had to bear the cost of replacing these parts twice as frequently as expected. Ultimately, of course, they had to fix the component design.

At the start of the project, the team noticed a few things. First, as they saw the "cost of making a change" curve, they immediately recognized how expensive it is to discover the failure when the devices were in the hands of their customer. This got them to talking about what it would take to mitigate the risk that this could happen again.

They looked at their test plan. Their tests went to great lengths to confirm that the chip fab machine did what it was supposed to do. But they were not driving it to the point of failure. They realized the test systems were so expensive that they only built and tested a single etch chamber mechanism. Nobody would have dared to requisition a second one. But after getting clear on the actual cost of the previous project's failure, the project manager and the lead engineer looked at the budget to build test versions of the hardware, crossed out "one etch chamber subsystem" and replaced it with "three." Our job, they said, is not simply to make sure the system works to spec. Our customer is going to work the device to failure; therefore, it is critical that we test it to failure first. If these components don't get destroyed by our testing, then our testing isn't complete.

Organizations that take on projects that involve building expensive infrastructure, hardware, tooling, have big technology expenses, or involve expensive physical experiments usually have a few key features such as these:

♦ The organization often has established and dedicated groups that provide project management.

♦ The project management team is expected to drive the project through specific "phase gates" that control the expenditure of capital. Projects need to prove to management at these specific points in time that they have accomplished certain objectives to merit financing of the next phase. Capital **commitment** ramps up phase by phase, often by orders of magnitude.

♦ Products, after they've been bought by the customer, often have considerable ongoing expense associated with manufacturing, operation, support, warranty, and so on.

Such projects have a very steep "cost of making a change" curve. They benefit the most from a rigorous shift of change toward the front end of the project. To accomplish that, we want to emphasize a few aspects of Risk Up Front.

Properly filling out the core team at the beginning is critical. The team must include all the aspects of the project that contribute to operational costs. This means Manufacturing and Support need to be in the room from the very beginning. The team should expect to be making a 5W tradeoff that explicitly acknowledges the costs and risks of manufacturing and support. Initial "Design for Manufacturing" and "Design for Serviceability" reviews should be happening during the **commitment phase**.

A capital-intensive project may run for more than a year. Recognize that it is human nature at the start of such a project to manifest your internal "optimistic procrastinator." This often shows up as "We have plenty of time to bring in Support Team representatives later, when we are ready to start thinking about support."

Your support and manufacturing teams are probably 110 percent busy with day-to-day operations and cannot be expected to volunteer to strengthen the start of your project without significant management insistence. Creating a culture in which projects begin with a fully cross-functional **core team** is a significant act of will on the part of the leaders of the project. You won't be able to tell these team members what they need to do at the beginning because those things are in the team's **blind spot**. They must be there in order to move the blind spot.

Recognize that the boundaries within your organization are not the boundaries of an effective cross-functional project team. Critical members of your team will be outside your product group. Organizational silos invariably get in the way. They are often not only organizationally distant but also geographically remote. The engineering team members often don't have regular opportunities to meet with and establish relationships with members from areas such as sales, manufacturing, and support. The lack of free-flowing communication across organizational boundaries both hides and exacerbates the risks that lurk within your project.

Organizational separation creates risks that need to be explicitly acknowledged and mitigated. Different **track** members on your **project team** have deep expertise in their areas, and they don't know how to talk to one another. They use different language for their operation and environment. Training them on the principles of Risk Up Front gives them a common vocabulary language to define objectives and, most importantly, discuss risks. We have seen team members focused on the product support light up when they realize they can provide engineers with cause, effect, and impact and see them understood and acted on.

Do not drown the core team in low-risk project detail. Complex, capital-intensive projects generate a lot of day-to-day information, such as lab results, design tests, customer feedback, and more. We often see large cross-functional project reviews spend too much meeting time buried in their review of data. Don't let this happen. Focus your cross-functional meetings on risks and their mitigation. Separate technical reviews with a smaller audience may be required.

Test to failure. There is a natural, optimistic tendency to design tests of complex equipment to make sure that they do what the team has said they must do. Testers ensure that all the affirmative specifications are met—we call this Test to Pass. However, we know when you design a product to go to ten, the first thing your customer will do is dial it to eleven. Allocate time and resources to predict how your customers will abuse your product, then abuse it in your lab first. We call that Test to Fail—and you want to do more of it.

Focus on removing barriers to starting the next phase gate. If your project governance uses phases and phase gates, acknowledge that aspects of the work associated with different phases will overlap. Instead of focusing on what it takes to complete a given phase, focus on what blocks the start of the next phase. Get those blocks out of the way. Do the least necessary to enter the next phase—and no less. Make sure all the remaining work in a previous phase is eventually verified complete.

Leverage the WAM to rapidly communicate project state. Keep it tight. Teams on large projects are pleasantly surprised at how the **WAM** agenda lets them communicate the state of the project, the performance of the team, the robustness of their **commitment**, and the identification of risks faster and better than they imagined was possible. They are used to the town hall presentations that share the details of the project, that focus on the tsunami of information rather than the proactive identification of risk.

Because of that, it is very important to drive the entire team through each **WAM** with both rigor and velocity. This takes a very firm hand on the part of the facilitator. The "top two risks" conversation in the **WAM** should give a transparent insight into the project to the entire **core team**.

Very large projects require a hierarchy of teams, fully cross-functional at the top. As a project team grows in size and complexity, we see track leaders gathering their own subteams to manage the deliverables of their track. The track leader, in consultation with the project lead, will identify those deliverables that are appropriate to put on the RUF weekly schedule to track at the core team level in the WAM.

Some track leaders like to rotate whom they choose to be their lieutenant over the course of the project. That's fine. The important thing is that someone other than the track leader needs to be on the core team, so she is up to speed if she needs to take over the leadership of her track for any reason and also to ensure that information is conveyed back reliably from the core team to the subteams.

KEY RECOMMENDATIONS

♦ Involve the entire **cross-functional project team**, including representatives from the sales, support, and manufacturing organizations, from the beginning of the project. Their role at the beginning is to identify and work with the engineering team to mitigate risks that will manifest themselves months later when the project falls in their lap.

♦ Focus large cross-functional meetings on identifying risks. Don't let them devolve into problem solving. If you have thirty people watching two people discuss a problem, your meeting has probably fallen down a rat hole.

♦ When prioritizing results during a given project phase, focus on what prevents the next phase from beginning.

♦ When designing test plans, budget resources to test through failure. Plan on breaking expensive units of hardware in the test lab so you're not surprised when they break at the customer site.

CHAPTER 11

DISTRIBUTED TEAMS:
SPANNING GEOGRAPHIES, TIME ZONES, LANGUAGES, AND CULTURES

The business manager (who happens to be French) has called for a project review, which includes designers and business leaders from the United States, China, and Japan.

They had all been trained in Risk Up Front. In fact, getting this cross-functional group onto airplanes to gather in one room, face-to-face, was specifically identified by the business manager as a necessary risk mitigation activity the teams in his business unit required. At this meeting, the *risk action plan* was projected on the wall, as it was at nearly every team meeting.

At one point, the Chinese design team leader got up to present one of the design elements he was worried the business team wasn't clear on. Because he was presenting in English, which was not his native language, he had prepared a ten-minute detailed presentation about the risk—he wasn't confident, given his limited English, that they'd "get it" without that level of detail.

As he began, the business manager asked him to pause and then pointed to one of the items on the risk list. The manager asked the engineer to simply read aloud the cause, effect, and impact recorded for that risk, just as his team had written it. That done, the room was quiet for a moment.

> Articulating the cause, effect, and impact was all that was necessary to have the US managers "get it." The remainder of their conversation was not about communicating the risk but rather how they would work together to mitigate it.

It is now common for us to be pulled into projects that involve participants spread around the globe. On these projects, we notice some aspects of the environment reappear over and over. Here are some things to consider:

Acknowledge and mitigate risks of low-quality communication channels. Team members in different time zones (such as India and the United States) are most often communicating asynchronously (e.g., via email exchange) and through "low bandwidth" channels such as conference calls.

Establishing team norms across cultural boundaries is still necessary, and it takes extra focus. It's hard to make cultural norms around project behavior stick. Even if the whole team gets together and talks about how they want to approach their project, when individuals get back to their home turf, the "local" culture and behavioral norms often reemerge. This becomes a problem when those local norms are inconsistent with team agreements and override them.

Recognize that splitting a team across geographies is a choice. While defining your project, account explicitly for both the upside and the downside of this choice. Make sure risks associated with this choice are identified and mitigated. One of the main issues we come up against is that organizations rapidly understand and appreciate the cost reduction, increased productivity, and flexibility associated with splitting projects among teams in different locations. Even so, we must push them to quantify those things. More important, they underappreciate the increased risk and added complexity of splitting projects in that manner. If you can collect your team in one location, you can remove those risks and complexities. But even when you can't, we have found the simplicity and rigor of Risk Up Front provides a simple way to span the cultural and geographic divides that exist within project teams to effectively mitigate those risks. A few aspects of Risk Up Front become critical.

Gather your dispersed team into one place for up-front training and kickoff. All members of the **cross-functional project team** should be trained in the terminology of Risk Up Front, with team members from different geographies collected in the same room. As a side effect, team members will get to know one another face-to-face, which will pay big dividends when they have to understand one another over low-bandwidth calls and emails later in the project.

We encourage, in our training, non-English-speaking teams to discuss the RUF "reserved words" in their own language. It is inspiring to see them argue about what word or phrase properly captures the nuances they know they need to capture. To have that argument in front of their English-speaking peers is a great reminder that the amount of mental energy it takes to wrestle with abstractions such as **accountability, transparency, integrity**, and **commitment**.

If you're not sure when to get on a plane, focus travel on meetings to identify and mitigate risk. In the absence of Risk Up Front, it may be unclear what team members should get on a plane for. With RUF, at least one case becomes clear: get people on planes for the critical DKDK meetings. Thus, for definition meetings, get people on planes. Again, the face-to-face interaction among the team members here will set the culture that can be leveraged later when communication bandwidth is lower. For the **WAM**, it may be workable to use video-conferencing to get everyone looking at one another. In any case, we firmly recommend that if you can't get your project done with a **core team**'s participation in these meetings, then restructure the project so it can be completed successfully by a team that can.

Investing in having the cross-geography team meet in the same room early in the project for training and definition meetings will avoid costly emergency flights around the world later in the schedule.

Make sure RUF project documents are effectively communicated throughout the entire project team, even across boundaries and languages. Require that at minimum, the Risk Up Front **project documents**, those four pieces of paper, be translated into the common team language. Depending on the project, there will usually be a few other key documents that should also be in the common language, such as a product backlog or engineering designs. All geographies should have access to the master versions of these **project documents** so the changes are all made and can be transparently seen in one place. Team members may keep their personal documents and lab notes in their local language, but they will be clear that information and issues that must be communicated team-wide will need to be shared in a standard, agreed-upon manner.

The ideas of Risk Up Front resonate across the globe. When we work with multilingual teams whose native language is not English, we include a simple exercise in our training: "Translate the Risk Up Front definitions for **transparency**, **accountability**, **integrity**, and **commitment** into your native language." This starts a fascinating discussion, as the participants wrestle with the nuances of the definitions that make the principles real and useful on their teams.

At a workshop for one of our clients in Shenzhen, China, we added a slide the team created, describing the Chinese phrases their own teams use to dismiss risk discussions:

这事不该我管.	This is not my job.
说了也没用.	There's no use saying it.
以前都是这样子啊.	It used to happen a lot.
老板会不喜欢.	My boss doesn't care.
这样会得罪人.	It would offend/displease someone.
负责的人都不在.	I'm not the person in charge.
下班了·明天再说.	We're off work; let's wait until tomorrow.

Fig. 34: Risks as complaints, Chinese edition.

Because language is a lever to shift culture and behavior, working with teams to engage with the concepts and tools of RUF in their native language is both powerful and fun.

Meeting facilitation of video and audio conference calls requires special skill and care. During such meetings, facilitators need to be extremely careful to make sure people on the far side of a video link, or team members attending from afar who may have language or cultural barriers to overcome, are given full participation in the meeting. A common breakdown occurs when a facilitator allows a meeting structure to slide over some requirement to accommodate a team member who doesn't speak the meeting language fluently. For example, in a **WAM**, ALL participants are expected to state two risks. It may be tempting to let this requirement slide, but don't do it. Respect one another's contribution by giving them the space and support to provide what every other team member is expected to provide. If this requires accommodations (translators, advance preparation, or other support), we encourage teams to make those accommodations. Practices that require everyone's participation are very useful and should be started early in the project.

Have team members submit their two risks in writing before the WAM. A modification to the **WAM** that distributed teams have found useful is to require team members to submit their "top two risks" in a slide (one per team member) prior to the **WAM**. The slide can be projected while each team member reads their top risks. These "supertitles" for the risk conversation serve two purposes: (1) it makes it easier for non-native speakers to follow along because reading the risk may be easier than hearing it on a call, and (2) prior to the meeting, it pushes team members to be better prepared at clearly articulating their risks and to get help if they have issues with language.

KEY RECOMMENDATIONS

♦ Spreading a project across geographies always creates risks. Make sure you rigorously account for those risks and mitigate them. When you can make the **5W trade-off** on your project so it can be done successfully in one location, you remove these risks—although it may create others.

♦ RUF training and definition meetings should be done with the team in one room. If you get team members on planes for anything, get them on planes for this. It will pay large dividends later in the project.

♦ For video conferences that span geographies (e.g., for a **WAM**), project the project document driving the meeting—for example, the **weekly schedule**—so all participants can see it during the meeting.

♦ Master copies of key **project documents** must be readable by every team member in every geography. They must be synchronized and up to date. Solve your document-sharing problem.

♦ Leverage the rigor of language tools such as the CEI form and the structure of the **project statement** to help team members whose native language is not the team's common language.

CHAPTER 12

STARTUP COMPANIES

A startup company formed to resell telecom services (they were a "competitive local exchange carrier," or CLEC) was working on their individual accountabilities as part of a RUF project definition.

As part of the company's operational process, one of the employees, along with her other duties, was tasked with ordering bandwidth. She placed those orders, as needed, with their telecom provider (the "incumbent local exchange carrier," or ILEC). Those orders have a six-to-eight-week lead time, as they involve the physical installation of fiber cable as well as hardware changes in the local switch.

Just a few weeks before we started working with their team, that woman left the company. Nobody thought much about it; everything continued to run well. However, when we did the exercise for establishing individual accountabilities, it became clear that (1) getting those orders placed was an important thing, and (2) no one had been placing the orders since she had left the company. With the chaos of the startup, with people coming and going, this had not been noticed. The mitigation was easy—the task was given a new owner, the orders were placed, and the bandwidth was available when their customers needed it.

The CEO told us this catch saved them hundreds of thousands of dollars. For their startup, this was critical.

Startup companies are fun and exciting. But if you haven't been at a startup company, it's hard to imagine the level of chaos and stress that allows "obviously" important things to go unnoticed. When working with startups, we notice a few common threads:

♦ Team members are new to one another. This doesn't mean they are inexperienced; there may be deep expertise among the team members. But whether they are experts, they haven't worked together as a team. They often bring different cultural norms and practices from their previous experiences. Teams that have histories of working together have settled on workflow or process optimizations that work for them based on their experience. New teams don't have that benefit.

♦ Projects at startups are generally not "incremental." Whatever they are building, it is "version 1." Often, it is breaking new ground, either utilizing a novel technology, disrupting an existing market, or creating an entirely new product category. It is not surprising that many risks are identified and prioritized super-high: "No one has ever done this before."

♦ It is quite common for startup teams to be entirely lacking in a subject matter area that they'll need. Their project starts before they are fully staffed. For example, they may not have any salespeople on board when they start building their product, or they may not have expertise in a very special technical area.

When we work with these teams to implement Risk Up Front, there are a few issues that commonly arise.

Notice where you're missing expertise, and deal with it creatively. Startups often avoid planning because they do not know enough to plan—they just dive in. By thinking carefully about what they want to trade off, they discover how going through a RUF **commitment phase** aligns the team and, most importantly, uncovers risks even though certain tracks are yet unstaffed on the team. They often don't realize the importance of bolstering key areas of expertise to even define their project. For example, one of our clients hired a sales consultant to stand in for their not-yet-hired sales team, so they could have useful conversations about whom their customers might be and how they would sell against their competition. Developing a shipping product is different than developing just the technology.

Manage integrity from the beginning. For a new team coming together, you cannot assume that trust will arise spontaneously. But you can engineer it into your team using RUF. The process of getting a team together to discuss risks from the beginning and to manage their **integrity** from the beginning creates an early environment in which people feel heard and act with greater **integrity**—they are more reliable in keeping promises. This is the base from which we see trust emerge.

Often, newly formed teams don't realize that deploying tools leads to team rituals that can make a huge difference. The key is to use these simple tools with rigor.

By making the state of the project, including its risks, rigorously transparent, it is easier for startups to pivot. Startup companies are often faced with the need to pivot. In other words, they realize their current direction is not going to take them to the level of profitability they need to survive. Risk Up Front helps teams notice their lack of progress earlier. Risks identified early will escalate if initial mitigations are unsuccessful. If that fails, the fact that there is an articulated outcome, a clear direction, shared throughout the team, means the team has a common shared base to pivot from. It is much easier for a company to change direction when all the participants are very clear on the direction they were going before the pivot, and clear that the risks associated with that direction have not been successfully mitigated.

For startups, time spent up front identifying and mitigating risks is a matter of survival. We occasionally see two areas of resistance that come up when introducing startup teams to RUF. The first is that there is often a significant bias against "taking time." The reason many people join a startup is because there is an idea they are fascinated with, but that is often only a piece of making a successful product or business. The team doesn't have the luxury of letting that be "someone else's responsibility." There is no "someone else." It takes strong leadership to push such a team into the room together, to realize that there are things they don't know they don't know, and the company cannot afford to let them remain hidden.

The bottom line is that the super-high risks for a startup company are existential risks. The company cannot survive spending all its capital to build a product and then discover that that product has a fatal flaw. There's no capital left to pay to fix it.

Balance the various tracks in your project team and focus on productive internal negotiation. The startup team is often very heavy in one area of its organization. Some startups are "engineering first." They have an engineering team and very weak marketing, operations, or sales teams. Or they might be "marketing first." They don't have any development or engineering experience—they're going to outsource all that. These imbalances make it relatively hard to get into action to identify and mitigate risks because the team first must acknowledge that they must somehow fill those gaps early, or they'll get bitten by risks later.

After filling those gaps, we then see marketing teams and engineering teams all making big plans based on little real-world experience. Marketing asks for the moon, and engineering is afraid to make commitments. Project priorities turn into wish lists. The RUF framework, especially the conversations around risk priorities (e.g., "Has anyone done this before?" versus "Have we done this before?") keep the team realistic about what they can and cannot initially deliver. Marketing, from the start, is taught to take engineering commitments (and their inability to commit) seriously, and Engineering is taught to understand carefully the market concerns that stand between a successful product and a flop.

Leverage RUF to establish the culture you want to survive initial churn and eventual growth. Perhaps the most important benefit for startups using Risk Up Front is that it gives them a forum to establish the culture they want for their company early on. We often hear this from startup founders who are growing their businesses rapidly, and suddenly their team went from a few friends to a group of people who don't know one another. The forum to talk seriously about cultural norms—not a natural conversation for many of us—turns out to be incredibly important. New team members arrive into an environment that already has a culture of **accountability**, **transparency**, **integrity**, and **commitment**, along with the tools to measure those things. Instead of bringing their old habits into a vacuum, there is a stable cultural norm they can latch on to that makes them immediately a member of the team.

KEY RECOMMENDATIONS

◆ Use RUF as part of your process for establishing norms of culture and ritual at your startup, especially around your expectations for **transparency**, **integrity**, **accountability**, and **commitment**. Let newcomers arrive into an environment where these norms are clear and settled.

◆ Account for all the areas of knowledge and expertise your project needs to deliver a commercially successful result. If you don't have staff to cover those areas, identify that explicitly as a risk, and decide how you're going to mitigate it.

♦ Leverage RUF projects beyond product development. Create "ninety-day projects" to build the company. The fiscal quarter can be structured as a project where the management team is the project team.

CHAPTER 13

SOFTWARE PROJECTS AND AGILE METHODOLOGY

Agile/Scrum methods are widely used for software development. *The Agile Manifesto* was published in 2001, and the book *Agile Development with Scrum* by Ken Schwaber and Mike Beedle, two of the signers of the manifesto, was written shortly thereafter. Most of the software teams we work with these days have adopted some version of the Agile/Scrum approach to developing their products. The following discussion assumes you are familiar with the basics.

> A small Silicon Valley company has raised the capital they need to build a cutting-edge graphics platform for media companies. They have gotten together an extraordinary team and had produced a compelling demo. Their CEO, who had worked with Risk Up Front in previous startups, was impressed by the Agile process the team had put in place—they had compiled an interesting backlog of activity to move the demo forward and were burning that backlog down.
>
> What they didn't have was a product, and the CEO knew it. We were asked to get "unstuck," to help the team transition from demo to product.

Many of the key aspects of Risk Up Front, particularly the focus on *transparency* and *commitment* are emphasized in Scrum. The team needed little coaching to upgrade their behavior with respect to these principles. But what they quickly realized was that while they were going through the motions of grooming their backlog and burning through it week by week on their sprints, they couldn't step outside that loop to identify what they wanted their product to be nor did they have a sense of who their customer was. In fact, it was a significant epiphany when they discovered they needed to be able to speak about "the project to complete a product," as opposed to "getting the software done."

This came about in an unexpected way. We held the first *definition meeting*, beginning with the first conversation about the "target customer." They all had a general idea about who the target customer might be, but the act of having to clearly define it surfaced important disagreements and identified hard decisions they realized had to be made immediately.

Because they'd been trained on the RUF approach for articulating risks, one of the first risks they identified was that no one was accountable for the "entire product." Everyone assumed the senior engineering lead was also the *project leader*, but when all the non-software measures of success were drafted, it became clear that the CEO needed to manage the project—at their startup stage, there was no one else positioned to do so. Suddenly, the CEO realized that this needed to be his role. The crucial problem was not how to organize the backlog of work into a product; it was to have someone in the room on the hook for there being a salable product.

It is common when we're working with software groups that they are decidedly *not* cross-functional. The Agile and Scrum processes, as they are often adopted, force a narrow "club-biness" on teams. They stand up every morning, make their commitments to one another, and the focus is intense and often short term: what is the problem in front of us, and how will we get it out of our way. There is rarely any conversation that might discover an important perspective is missing. After all, stand-up meetings are led and run typically by engineers—they pride themselves on solving whatever problem is put in front of them.

In the language of RUF, Agile incorporates no strong practice for the team members to uncover their **blind spots.**

We want to reiterate that Agile is an incredibly productive tool for developing software. But for teams committed to building products that make their *business* successful, we want to add a few things to the mix.

Establish an overall project arc, with a clear project definition and a valuable result. Most importantly, we need to create a project arc overlaying the sprints of the team. This arc must be designed explicitly by the team to end with a commercially valuable result that includes all the functional groups necessary for product success. In addition to the daily stand-up meetings, add a **weekly accountability meeting** where all the functions attend, track weekly deliverables and communicate top risks. The software team can select key deliverables in their sprints that are tracked and accounted for in the **weekly schedule**. We find teams often discover that developing the software may not be the riskiest activity for a commercial product. Securing partnerships or effective user training may be the most difficult project deliverables.

Risk conversations are necessary and must be cross-functional. Explicitly introduce conversations about risk. One of the most useful things an Agile team can do when they take on a RUF **commitment phase** is to look at their backlog and assign a RUF risk priority to each item. Remember, the RUF risk prioritization is focused on the team's experience level with a risk. Software teams will mistakenly assume items are not difficult even though they have no experience in that area. Then two things invariably happen:

Because the impact conversation of risks is by definition the "impact on the business," the conversation changes from what may or may not work (at the software level) to what money the company might lose. This forces the conversation about the business value of the project.

Instead of burning down the backlog in the order of "easy things first," which allows the team to easily score high "velocity" (which Scrum teams are trying to maximize), we focus the team on tackling necessary but risky backlog items first. We want to force potential changes to be discovered early when those changes are less expensive. In practice, about 10 percent of the backlog may be moved around as a result of this analysis.

Get specific about the commercial impact of risks. Managers are often trained by their Agile teams to "leave the team alone." The team takes the position that by reporting their high velocity, management should understand that the team is making adequate progress. But as we know, velocity is not speed alone—it is speed *and* direction. If the team does not have accountable experts on what the direction (result) of the project should be, you, as a manager, have a right to be skeptical of the actual value of their progress. As you are listening to the team's conversations about their project risks, make sure they are able to get specific and measurable about business impacts. If they can't, that is evidence of a blind spot.

Introduce sufficient cross-functional participation. Finally, we push teams to consider that their teams are probably not sufficiently cross-functional. We want them to solve problems by pulling in the right people, with the right accountabilities, and make them first-class members of the project team. If the software project is inside a large company, this often means reaching across silos and organizational boundaries. If the project is at a startup, this may mean pulling in an outside consultant or adviser to stand in for the eventual hire.

KEY RECOMMENDATIONS

♦ Focus on creating profit, not creating software.

♦ If you use an Agile/Scrum approach for software development, note that RUF augments these; it does not replace them.

♦ Assign RUF risk priorities ("Have we done it before?") to elements of your backlog. Order your backlog for a given project by risk priority, and schedule risky items earlier.

♦ Overlaying your sprints, create project boundaries that have a clear start and a commercially valuable end point.

♦ Start your projects with a commitment phase that includes a complete cross-functional project team, covering all the required tracks. The first few sprints should be about resolving issues and mitigating risks that are in the way of exiting the commitment phase.

♦ Using RUF alongside Agile, you will still find yourself integrating customer requirement changes over the course of your sprints. That is the heart of Agile. But because doing so late in the project is expensive, you'll incorporate up-front activity that will result in fewer late changes.

CHAPTER 14

INFORMATION TECHNOLOGY:

IN-HOUSE PROJECTS

The IT Department of a large utility company has been tasked with rolling out a new Human Resources support system for their tens of thousands of employees to manage their benefits. The project team had identified a system from a major vendor they'd customize to provide online HR support.

As they began to answer the basic questions required to draft the project statement, they realized the real goal that was interesting to the company was not just a working online HR system but one that would effectively reduce the number of calls to HR support staff (replacing them with self-service via the new system). They also realized in their large nontechnical workforce that the highest risk they faced was not that they'd fail to deploy the system but rather that employees would still find it easier to pick up the phone, as they always had, than to use a new automated system.

In fact, what they thought was a software problem was largely a training problem. To succeed, they had to teach a large nontechnical population how to use the system and to prefer it over calling the HR help desk. Their measures of success shifted. They were no longer focused on a "working software system." Instead, they aligned the team around delivering a "reduction in calls to HR staff."

> They determined one of the key components on their project was a well-designed and fully implemented training program, along with the plan to roll it out. They then discovered the critical missing team resource in the definition meeting was not an engineer; it was an accountable team member from the training department.

IT Departments sit within large companies to provide development services and operational support for the technology and systems that allow their companies to operate efficiently. They are not building the products the company sells, yet the company could not provide those products and services without this IT support.

Effort is often wasted on successful delivery of unsuccessful results. The landscape of back office projects is littered with large development efforts that succeeded at delivering large systems that turn out to be unused. On the one hand, the IT team feels they were successful—they delivered their software, on time, under budget. On the other hand, it was a colossal waste of effort.

Tie project success to commercial benefit, even for in-house projects. One of the reasons this happens is that management does not force the team to settle on measures of success that represent value to the company. In the anecdote above, the shift from "deploy a system" to "reduce HR staff support cost" is a common example of this shift from a frame that is natural to the engineering team to a frame that is valuable to the company.

Even when such a project considers the ultimately valuable "increased productivity" or "reduced cost" they provide, this thinking is often fuzzy—it is not specific and measurable. If you are on such a project, push your team to identify measurable savings (real numbers!) that would make the project worthwhile to do. This will help in your budgeting process and in internal negotiations with business units. It also improves morale. Engineers like to see their systems used.

Choose a target customer that will deliver the commercial benefit. This often comes up in **definition meetings** when the team is discussing who is the **target customer**. At our utility company, the IT team at first considered the HR Department to be their only target customer. They then realized that given their newly framed measures of success, that the company workforce was also an important target customer.

We often push even further and ask the internal development team to identify how their project results impact that organization's external paying customers. Are you building something that reduces cost? That enables a higher level of support? That provides quantifiable operational efficiencies? Can the organization charge more or pay less to provide its product or service, given this addition to their infrastructure? An important commercial objective of the new HR system at the utility was the ability to facilitate mergers and acquisitions that would deliver value to customers and shareholders. If the team can identify these benefits and, more importantly, measure them, then it is more obvious how much money and time should be spent on getting that internal project executed.

Internal projects, especially information technology projects, serve companies better when they are tied to profit,

rather than cost. An internal team can shift from being an isolated cost of the organization to being an integral part of the organization's profitability. The technology the internal team is providing should make the company more profitable. Focusing on this end goal will push the team to engage in conversations across a wider cross-section of the organization about what is truly useful. This makes it less likely they will spend their effort on outcomes that seem successful from their local vantage point but are not valued by the business.

KEY RECOMMENDATIONS

◆ Be careful about how you think of the **target customer** and **customer measures of success** for your project. Start with the premise that internal projects have an important impact on external customers. Whenever possible, set your project goal to include a measurable improvement in the profitability of the company.

◆ When articulating **business measures**, focus on specific, measurable improvements in reducing costs and increasing revenues, rather than just changes in efficiency or productivity.

◆ Center your project definition on what you need to *enable*, not (initially) on what you need to build. Most IT projects are thinly veiled organizational change projects. The world is full of fully implemented software packages that are not used within a company.

- Let your risk identification range broadly—not just what might impede the development and deployment of an internal tool or process, but what might block its adoption, what might render it obsolete, what might cause it to be operationally too expensive to operate or maintain, and so forth. The key is to pull in the people who know how to solve those kinds of problems early. They may not be on your engineering team.

- Be prepared to cross organizational boundaries ("silos") to build the proper cross-functional project team that you need.

CHAPTER 15

ORGANIZATIONAL CHANGE PROJECTS

A global multibillion-dollar enterprise software company had recently consolidated its financial technology businesses under one organization and introduced a new brand under which all the products would be sold. The objective of this consolidation was to offer a complete menu of products and services to their financial institution clients. New marketing material was created, new organizational charts were developed, and press releases were issued.

Almost a year later, not much had changed in the day-to-day running of the various product groups. The new brand was rarely mentioned in meetings, there was little cross-selling, and there had been little integration of the product development, sales, or customer-support activities.

Employees identified with their old organizations. People were using their old business cards with outdated branding, and there was little cross-selling. The company was not getting a return on its investment in integrating these disparate businesses. It looked like a failed merger.

It was clear to the head of the business group that the integration of his business units had stalled. He therefore decided to create a Risk Up Front organizational change project. He called together a project team that intentionally crossed his organizational silos. The team spanned functions, business units, and geographic areas—New York, Boston, Chicago, Paris, and Pune. It included both junior and senior managers, as well as individual contributors. He was able to accomplish that level of diverse representation with a team of fewer than thirty people. The team took on the mission to change their organization in ninety days.

As part of their project, they formed small working groups, each of which took on a key business function that had to be fixed (or eliminated). These working groups were never more than five people. Even though they were small, it was important each group included subject matter experts as well as representatives who spanned business units and functions.

By the end of ninety days, they had sorted out a couple dozen changes in personnel, processes, and tools. These changes were rolled out, with training as required, and selected changes were piloted to test and refine them.

Not only had the team achieved 93 percent of their defined goals for this project, but the act of taking on these issues in the working group structure allowed the team members to establish new working relationships across the entire business group. Those new connections were arguably the most important outcome of the project.

Applying Risk Up Front to organizational change efforts is an effective way to make real change quickly and ensure it sticks. Although you may not be used to structuring such activity in the form of projects, we find that applying Risk Up Front to organizational change yields particular benefits. We call this approach "project-based change."

These types of projects are especially powerful when "continuous improvement" efforts have stalled, or when a team or organization needs a jump start. They are a great way to engage a team after an organizational disruption such as a layoff, reorganization, or merger. They are also good for jumpstarting a new organization, such as a startup. Organizational change projects are useful in making discrete, measurable improvements on issues the organization believes are important, yet previously seemed intractable. These are often issues discussed around the coffee machine where there is agreement that "We really should do something about them," but a year later, nothing has been done.

We also recommend implementing project-based change projects when you need a way to do task-oriented team building within functional groups. Such projects provide an effective opportunity for colleagues who do not normally work together to join in an effort that fixes long-standing morale-busting issues in their environment. This can supplement, or even replace, traditional team-building activities—you know, rope courses, wine tasting, and so on (of course, we would never want to argue against wine tasting).

On your organizational change project, Risk Up Front tools are used to define the objectives, to engineer accountability and transparency into the conversations, and, of course, to effectively drive the project to success. It is important to build the project team from all the related business units or functional groups and to make sure all the affected geographies are represented. Team members will be identifying and setting in motion organizational changes. There are four types of people we expect to see on your team: critical subject matter experts, managers who will own the result, people for whom organizational improvement is a passion, and key stakeholders who may themselves be reluctant to implement proposed changes.

These projects provide an important opportunity to have individual contributors work with senior managers. The benefits of this "skip-level" interaction go both ways: frontline contributors become better acquainted with the intentions of top management, and senior managers get exposure to what is happening on the ground.

Organizational change projects require an executive sponsor who is the senior manager of the organization, typically the CEO or general manager. In larger businesses, the executive sponsor might be a vice-president of sales or engineering. The **project leader** should be a senior manager, individual contributor, or project manager with enough experience and expertise to lead a complicated project.

Prior to the first **definition meeting**, the project leader will prepare a first draft of the project statement. We recommend a few wording changes. Rename "target customers" to "target stakeholders" and expand that section of the project statement to include specific internal groups ("supply chain," "accounting"). You may also need to refer directly to individuals by name ("Jim, the head of our consumer banking group").

The **business measures** section of this first draft is critical. It sets the context for all the working groups. One of our clients, an electronic device manufacturer, anchored their project team with these simple yet powerful business measures: "Achieve 50 percent market share" and "Achieve profitability in Q2." These goals established the context that allowed the team to prioritize issues to work on and the activities of the working groups.

When organizing your team, instead of tracks and **track leaders**, there will be **"working group" leaders**. At the first **definition meeting**, the assembled team should decide on a small set of issues, typically three to five, and form working groups comprised of core team members. Do not have any team member serve on more than two working groups. We have seen working groups with names such as "Integrate Manufacturing," "Cost Reduction," and "Onboarding." We love it when working groups get creative with their names. For example, one of our government clients, developing a program for local armed services veterans, called their working group "Rolling Thunder."

You should **time box** these projects from the beginning. This also anchors the working groups. The job of each working group is to make a meaningful difference in their area, with specific and measurable deliverables, in the allotted block of time. A good time-boxed schedule for project-based change should run sixty to one hundred days. Size the objectives to the

> **Time box:** A *project definition* strategy that focuses on defining your project scope given a fixed project duration, rather than estimating your end date given a scope.
>
> You start with the question, "What is a reasonable amount of time to spend on this," and then consider the question, "What is the most useful thing to accomplish in the budgeted time?"

schedule. Remember, you can do another sixty-day project after. This is organizational change in "sprints."

The working groups will define their measures of success and components, which, in turn, flow up into the **project statement**.

Organizational change projects should explicitly use Risk Up Front's **"levers of culture"** model and identify which levers need to be changed to shift the organization in a new direction. The working groups should look for ways they can change the language, metrics, structures, and practices of their organization to impact its culture and operation.

After the first definition meeting, the working groups will meet separately to develop their own "working group" definition, trading off objectives, schedule, and resources as they need to. They will hold meetings to identify and mitigate their risks, and the working group leaders will run their own **weekly accountability meetings** for their groups. The project leader will meet with the working group leaders weekly to review progress and risks. A **weekly percent complete** is calculated for the entire project and communicated to the entire project team.

If there are dependencies among the objectives of different groups, the leaders will coordinate to work them out. At key milestones, the groups will present their status and risks to the entire project team. Otherwise, the working groups will manage themselves independently.

About a third of the way through the allotted **time box schedule**, the working groups should present the final draft of their plan to the entire project team. The **commitment phase** should end soon after that meeting, when the working groups have presented their objectives and the project team has confirmed their commitment.

Here are some specific examples from organizational change projects we have worked on. Notice how they directly address language, metrics, structures, and practices:

- At a semiconductor equipment manufacturer, one of the engineering functional groups had recently doubled in size. They were interested in building a higher level of teamwork among the old and new employees. In the resulting organizational change project, one of their working groups identified "customer escalations related to cable problems" as an important issue. They created and resourced a new cable configuration management system (structures) and reengineered their design reviews (practices) to reduce the frequency and cost of these escalations.

- At a software company, one of the working groups focused on creating a new customer engagement contract that would be used across their entire product group (structures) and defined new sales milestones that distinguish and track the value of cross-selling activity (language and metrics). Another working group, focused on employee onboarding, ordered business cards with new branding (language), and made sure that all departments in the organization received them (structures).

- One of our clients that manufactures optical transceivers reorganized from a functional structure into independent business units. The largest resulting business unit engaged in a ninety-day project to identify and implement critical cost reductions in their product (metrics, practices) and to more tightly integrate their California and China functional groups (language, structures, practices).

Span organizational and geographic boundaries when building your team to build relationships through which organizational change can get traction. Let the project serve as the "excuse" for pushing these key people to interact with one another effectively, taking responsibility for resolving organizational issues outside the requirements of their day-to-day interactions.

It is important to keep in mind these projects represent *an investment* in the key people in your organization. As individuals come together for an organizational change project, they will create a high-performance ad hoc team to make measurable progress toward inventing the future of your organization.

Our clients find the Risk Up Front approach applied to organizational change to be an excellent mechanism for allowing teams to initiate conversations on underlying issues in the organization. They will create a forum where team members can shake off their cynicism, resignation, and inertia, especially after difficult organizational transitions, by engaging in a quick, focused project that achieves meaningful improvements.

KEY RECOMMENDATIONS

♦ If you are in management, as the leader of a functional group or an entire business, and you know you need to address issues in your organization that have seemed intractable, execute an **organizational change project.**

♦ Use all the tools of **Risk Up Front,** including the four principles, the two meetings, and the four sheets of paper, to define and then execute your project.

♦ Organizational change projects using RUF should be between sixty and one hundred days in length.

♦ The schedule for the project should be defined at the beginning and objectives sized appropriately.

♦ Building relationships between key individuals across boundaries is an important result of an organizational change project. Strengthening these relationships will pay dividends in supporting the ongoing challenges of making change stick.

CHAPTER 16

NOT FOR PROFIT AND ELECTED GOVERNMENT OFFICES

Here's a project environment we don't see every day. A senior executive from one of our client companies, years after our engagement, was elected to the US Congress. He then reengaged us to coach his newly formed congressional office into a high-performing team.

> Military veterans in the congressman's district form a key constituency, and they have needs the congressman is committed to addressing. He and his staff believed an important service they could do for these vets was to help them transition into civilian jobs after their military service was complete. The team agreed a job fair for vets would be extremely valuable.
>
> However, a congressional office is busy with a wide variety of activities, including constituent services, consulting with colleagues and their staff, drawing up legislation, and preparing for important votes. The staff finds itself subject to a constant barrage of interruptions, which all seem like urgent emergencies.
>
> Just to hold the first job fair, there is a lot of work to do. Veteran organizations need to be involved as well as local and regional employers. There's advertising, logistics, recruiting, and scheduling

an appropriate venue. In the face of the constant demands on the staff, it is hard to make headway.

When we worked with them to implement Risk Up Front, the first thing they noticed is they had to isolate the job fair as a distinct project (they named it Rolling Thunder). In their first **definition meeting**, they realized a high risk was that team members would get sucked into the day-to-day problem solving of the office and would have no time to get the project done. They also realized because of the short time span of a congressional term, if they took too long to plan the job fair, they would not have time to adequately serve the vets in their district.

This shifted their thinking. They needed to make the job fair happen at the beginning of the congressional term, not at the end. It also became clear the job fair should not just be the responsibility of the veteran liaison staffer in the district office; a successful job fair required active involvement by the communications staff in DC and the constituent caseworkers in case there was follow-up. Defining clear accountabilities among these different offices allowed them to carve out an appropriate amount of their time, increased communication and coordination between the DC office and the field office, and made sure all the critical range of deliverables and risks were identified early.

By insisting on their own **integrity** and **commitment** to the project, they got all the logistics handled, and the first job fair took place. Several dozen vets showed up, a turnout they considered to be disappointingly low. But the staff now knew how to do this project, and the same team immediately scheduled the next job fair, adjusting their outreach. At the second job fair, there were about eighty vets. At the third, more than two hundred. By the time the first term ended, the veteran organizations and employers were happily taking advantage of these services and credited their congressman for his support.

The staff had organized itself around getting a nontrivial project done while the office operations continued. By identifying a *project leader*, the chief of staff was able to hold someone accountable for its success. He was able to get an end date the participants could commit to and force them to be honest about prioritizing their activity in the name of delivering on their commitments with *integrity*. The chief of staff also appreciated the recurring focus on risks, because it gave him a handle from outside the project team to help remove roadblocks brought to his attention early enough that he could intervene.

The congressman's team used RUF to manage other initiatives including economic development and support for the district's agricultural industry.

Having successfully deployed Risk Up Front on this project, the staff now uses these tools to isolate and execute specific projects for other goals that had previously languished. They pick them off and get them done.

We are fascinated by the issues at play when we were tasked with introducing a congressional office to Risk Up Front. The environment has many aspects different from those we normally see in the commercial world. The most obvious one is the congressman's time is constrained to distinct, two-year terms. While some members of Congress are guaranteed several terms, that is not true for all.

This means there is limited, high-quality feedback over the course of a term that informs you as to whether you are going to be reelected or not.

But there are other aspects of the environment that make it challenging. For example, you maintain at least two offices separated by geography, one in your district and a Washington, DC, office. Each is buffeted by its own pressures, with local constituents and institutions on the one hand and DC legislators and interest groups on the other.

The modern political environment exists at the whim of a 24-7 news cycle. There is a constant risk of a news event that will derail short-term plans, and it can happen at any time on any day. These often spur an "all hands on deck" response, even if they don't warrant it. These are not always negative—the news cycle does create opportunities. The common thread is, they are unpredictable and may derail commitments.

As our client began to learn the principles of Risk Up Front and think about how they would use it to improve their productivity and performance, a few things became clear.

Remap commercial concepts into those that are valuable to your organization. First, they had to identify measures of success that were measurable on a timetable sooner than the end of the term. They were quite clever in "remapping" the Risk Up Front concepts that businesses use. For example, on their **project statement**, the **target customers** section was renamed **stakeholders** (which include individual constituents, local businesses, unions, veterans, and other groups). **Customer measures of success** was renamed **stakeholder measures of success.**

But what, then, would **business measures** correspond to?

For the official office, the concept of business measures was renamed **stakeholder feedback**. So, for example, if the office provides a new constituent service, then measurable feedback might come in the form of calls to use that service. Or the local newspaper might write up a positive editorial, and that would be a measurable instance of positive stakeholder feedback.

Let work prioritization take the form of a competition among distinct projects with articulated costs, value, risks, and accountable individuals. The other important change in how they operated involved the identification of projects within the term and how they should be ordered. The offices had a history of creating **accountability** in the form of giving individuals ownership of particular "portfolios." For example, one staff member would own "veterans' issues," and another would own "agriculture." Each staff member had a set of portfolios she covered.

Every office decided what issues were most important to them. What was needed was an ability to take those issues and create distinct projects with cross-functional project teams that could deliver measurable results early in the term. RUF provided the framework to create defined projects and teams. Having defined, committed projects provided an important counterbalance to the often-overwhelming news cycle crisis response of the staff.

Having early, transparent conversations on project accountabilities allowed the team to spread those accountabilities more evenly across functions and between the DC and district office. For example, most projects have some communications component. Instead of having the communications director be a bottleneck on every project, another individual on the project team could take that **accountability** and would be responsible for making the communications team aware of what was needed and causing those things to get scheduled and executed. Instead of requiring that the communications team be everywhere and "pull" the needs from the office, project teams would "push" their needs to the communications team and do this early before it became a last-minute fire drill. This avoided the all-too-common scenario that starts with "Quick, we need a press release on an issue that we have never discussed before!"

Find activities that involve last-minute scrambling, and leverage RUF to push them to the front of a project. Of course, by creating these projects and running them through a **commitment phase**, teams raised risks early, and as their **blind spot** shrank, they noticed and discussed issues that had previously been ignored. They improved their internal and interoffice communication and morale. The increase in **transparency** created many additional opportunities for risk mitigation. An important side effect that was widely noted was that there were fewer fire drills. People who had work to do toward the end of the project, such as arranging for an event in the district, were apprised early on about what was coming down the pike, reducing the amount of last-minute scrambling.

Use RUF to identify and leverage areas of overlapping interest among otherwise disconnected parts of the organization. By establishing a set of project priorities that spanned both the local constituent-facing office and the DC legislature-facing office, there was a greater sense of partnership between these normally separated functions. The staff members in the two offices were able to see they were pulling toward the same set of objectives, and they were able to articulate concretely how those objectives achieved would improve the lives of their constituents and the country. The projects also gave them a regular opportunity to work across offices.

For the congressman whose story introduces this chapter, the culture of **accountability**, **transparency**, **integrity**, and **commitment** came to be admired by both constituents and colleagues. These RUF filters, language, metrics, structures, and practices were used throughout the activities of the office for both project and non-project work. Eventually, it was simply how the congressman and his staff operated. They have shared with us unexpected benefits that impressed them: reduced staff turnover, improved measurability of initiatives, increased number of laws proposed and passed. When interns join his team, they arrive into an organization that has an established and productive culture; in that environment, newcomers launch into projects with drive and enthusiasm.

KEY RECOMMENDATIONS

◆ In any noncommercial environment, you may need to "remap" some of the RUF concepts into those that make sense for your organization. In the congressman's office, this meant changing, "target customer" into "stakeholder," "customer measure of success" into "stakeholder measure of success," and "business measure" into "stakeholder feedback."

◆ Insist that measures of success are defined on your projects. Get creative to make them specific and measurable. What might you measure that you haven't measured before?

◆ Use the delineation of projects to serve as a counterweight to the day-to-day business of office operation.

◆ Pull into your projects parts of the organization that don't normally work together. Use the project structure to improve communication across functional and geographic boundaries.

◆ Because **accountability** is a causal role, be flexible about allowing team members to hold themselves accountable for things that are not specifically in their portfolio. They will not (necessarily) be on the hook to do the work; they will be on the hook to make sure it gets done as required by their project.

CHAPTER 17

TEACHING ENTREPRENEURSHIP:
UNIVERSITIES AND INCUBATORS

> We stood in front of a room of thirty undergraduate and graduate students assembled for a conference on teaching entrepreneurship. We asked a question, and only two hands went up. The question we had asked was, "Who considers themselves to be an entrepreneur?"
>
> We asked them why there were so few hands raised. Their response was, "We have not yet learned how to be entrepreneurs."

Entrepreneurship education has a problem. Imagine you are in an art school classroom, and you ask, "Who in the room is an artist?" Almost all hands would go up. "Entrepreneur" has become a title we give to people who are out in the world starting companies. The archetype entrepreneurs, such as Thomas Edison or Bill Gates, are often characterized by their lack of formal education, yet entrepreneurship curricula are becoming common in both traditional business schools and more novel environments, such as startup incubators and boot camps.

The business community struggles to determine whether entrepreneurship can be taught, let alone what *should* be taught.

Over time, the principles and processes of Risk Up Front have become the foundation of several innovative entrepreneurship programs at universities around the United States. Here's the story of two of these programs: the Lassonde Entrepreneurship Institute at the University of Utah and the nearby Foundry.

Rob Wuebker is a professor at the David Eccles School of Business at the University of Utah and one of the creators of the Foundry, an educational program and startup accelerator. He believes the narrow view of entrepreneurship embraced by academia misses a great opportunity to provide students with the entrepreneurial skills that will make them successful, regardless of whether they want to start and run their own business.

Wuebker uses Risk Up Front in the educational setting. His observation is students have easy access, between the internet and other settings, to learn the technical skills associated with starting a new business, such as how to write a pitch deck or how to set up a corporation. But to learn an entrepreneurial mindset, he has students learn and rigorously practice Risk Up Front principles and tools.

He believes RUF is a significant addition to the education landscape. A common refrain among funders of startups had been that entrepreneurship could not be taught to students. They felt the keys to entrepreneurial success were based in an individual's access to resources, rich peer networks, and the actual experience of running a business. Students have (generally) none of these things. So what's to teach?

What we find is that this world has changed. Today, the cost of building a product is collapsing. Globalization is allowing materials to be acquired cheaply and not only by large existing companies. Expertise can be found inexpensively around the world. All these factors change the basic calculation for students, and we see it ourselves—students come into our classrooms *already* executing their startup ideas.

These students come in with their product ideas and often well-developed technical skills. They've often learned (both in the classroom and from the internet) the basics of setting up collaborative efforts. They have often learned how to crowdsource funding for their projects. What happens when they go to a class on entrepreneurship?

Most of the focus in entrepreneur education, we find, is on external causes of startup failure. There is little emphasis on internal causes of failure. Founders believe that their company failures occur because they run out of money or resources, they don't have the right network, or they didn't get admitted to the right startup accelerator. When pressed, they might refer to their unfortunate decisions related to product market fit. In our view, their inability to drive themselves and their team to operate with **integrity** and **transparency** is one of the critical obstacles to creating successful companies.

Therefore, Risk Up Front is an important tool to be taught as part of a business or entrepreneurship curriculum. Risk Up Front serves as the fulcrum for students, allowing them to discover how to perform better and work faster. The entrepreneurial venture, the startup company, is the context in which they will apply those tools. Budding entrepreneurs using RUF can internalize core work behaviors that provide them more success in business, as they identify and address the entire spectrum of internal risks that might lead to business failure.

The Foundry

The Foundry was created in 2010 by University of Utah students as a response to learning **Risk Up Front** at the end of their entrepreneurship class. The students didn't want the class to end because they wanted to keep practicing RUF and get better at it to form new companies. They used their classmates as their team and met once a week to review their commitments and discuss the top two reasons their ventures would fail.

It started with eighteen students whose results defied the odds against success for such startups. What emerged were two or three high-growth businesses, employing 140 people or more. There have been several exits, and some of the students leapfrogged the traditional career path and are now executives in large established firms.

Skills that allow students to do work in ambiguous and unstructured contexts are the core behaviors that make startups work. By using the structures and practices of RUF and internalizing the concepts of **accountability, transparency, integrity**, and **commitment**, students discover these skills and hone them through self-discovery and actual use.

According to Wuebker, using RUF principles in the educational setting "is surprisingly powerful and surprisingly simple. You can teach it to middle school students. The techniques don't require high levels of life experience. The tools require very little in the way of education or entrepreneurial knowledge. There is no special software. It's basically 8.5" x 11" sheets of paper. It's low cost, easy, and really accessible."

Wuebker's program at the Foundry has drawn the attention of educators across the country. This is due in part to the unprecedented success of his students, who take three main tracks: the sole proprietor with a local business, the high-growth company, and the application of RUF principles and tools by junior employees in large companies.

Here is an example of a local business that was created by an undergraduate student in the first year of the Foundry. She created a small tax and accounting firm. Her goal while in school was to use her accounting skills as a basis to generate income to pay her tuition. She accomplished this and grew the company to five people. Today, her business is the main income for four other families. Although she could grow the business, she doesn't want to. She stopped her company's growth right where she wanted it and happily runs it while raising her family. She credits Risk Up Front with providing an organizational pattern in the very beginning that gave her business stability and continuity.

Wuebker notes, from a scholarly perspective, we don't know a lot about how to cause high-growth entrepreneurship. What we do know is the initial conditions at the founding of the company will influence its success twenty to thirty years out. Risk Up Front gives founders the tools they need in the beginning that gives their company a strong cultural and behavioral foundation for growth. One of the early Foundry success stories involved a beauty product company. The four founders came from other parts of the university and met at the Foundry. After a few unsuccessful attempts at forming a startup, the team hit on the idea brought to them by the wife of one of the founders—to build a business around selling nail appliqués and other beauty products. They tinkered with design and knew they were onto something when they sold out in two hours at their first trade show. They are now one of the fastest-growing direct-sales companies in the United States and have more than four hundred employees. They still use Risk Up Front to identify where they're going and what the risks are.

The third example is the application of entrepreneurial skills as core business skills. The students' RUF training gives them an advantage as they begin their careers. One student, after leaving the Foundry, started working in an entry-level position at a large commercial bank. He was phenomenally productive with his team. When asked how he made this happen, he introduced them to the tools of Risk Up Front. Even though he didn't specifically refer to the definitions and principles by name, he outperforms his peers by using the RUF **project documents**, the four sheets of paper. He is now an internal coach at the bank, improving their team's productivity.

The curriculum used by the Foundry has spread to a range of other educational institutions, and we are seeing startup incubators talk more and more about the importance of operationalizing **accountability, transparency, integrity,** and **commitment**.

KEY RECOMMENDATIONS

♦ Teach entrepreneurs how to create a RUF culture on their teams from the very beginning.

♦ Building a strong muscle for removing blind spots is a critical skill for entrepreneurs.

♦ RUF principles and tools can be taught in high schools and colleges. They are not just for "advanced" study in graduate programs and incubators.

♦ The only effective way to learn **Risk Up Front** is by using it on a project that matters to you and your team. Even in an academic setting, it can't be simply an academic exercise.

EPILOGUE

Anyway

People are often unreasonable and self-centered;
Forgive them anyway.
If you are kind, people may accuse you of selfish, ulterior motives;
Be kind anyway.

If you are successful, you will win some false friends and
some true enemies;
Succeed anyway.

If you are honest and frank, people may cheat you;
Be honest and frank anyway.
What you spend years building, someone could destroy overnight;
Build anyway.

If you find serenity and happiness, they may be jealous;
Be happy anyway.

The good you do today, people will often forget tomorrow;
Do good anyway.

Give the world the best you have, and it may never be enough;
Give the world the best you've got anyway.

You see, it was never between you and them anyway.
Only those who dare to fail greatly can ever achieve greatly.

– Based on *The Paradoxical Commandments*
by Dr. Kent M. Keith, 1968

It has been our privilege to work with extraordinary people on extraordinary teams over the past two decades. We realized early on while our work made a difference accelerating projects, what most affected us was the change in the teams themselves. As they increased their ability to work together, they were more honest, more direct, and happier with the work they were doing.

This is the argument for Risk Up Front: that taking a stand for accountability, transparency, integrity, and commitment is not just good behavior but is also the direct path to making your projects successful. It creates the kinds of teams on which we would want to work. We expect that you will, too.

It is not our intention that you minimize the risk on your projects. On the contrary, great teams take great risks. Our point is that they manage those risks rigorously. We'd like to leave you with a simple charge. Take the opportunity to work passionately on projects that matter to you, and as we said at the beginning of this book, always keep your sense of humor.

GLOSSARY

Much of the effect on Risk Up Front on teams stems from their careful and rigorous use of language. We consider such use to be the key to effective communication, the basis for measurable and productive **accountability**, **transparency**, **integrity**, and **commitment** on teams. These words should be read throughout the book using the definitions in the following glossary.

Most of our definitions are much more specific and precise than you would expect from the general sense of these words. In any area of specialization, we allow words to take on special meanings, and Risk Up Front is no exception. We train teams to understand and use this language. That is an important part of what makes them proficient practitioners of Risk Up Front.

In the definitions below, words in boldface are glossary words to be understood using their given definitions.

5

5W tradeoff

Trading off the Why, Who, What, When, and Why Not that define your project, to arrive at a project definition the **project team** can commit to. Every change to one of these axes changes what the project is. The goal of the **commitment phase** is to discover a **5W tradeoff** that makes sense and that the team can commit to deliver successfully.

A

Accountability

Singular ownership of a **result**. There is one member of the team who will cause the result, even if others are also involved. The rest of the team is aware of who this person is. Ensuring that accountabilities are clear is a useful way to uncover risks.

Accountability matrix

The RUF tool used to ensure that all the important results of the project have accountable owners, and to make this transparent to the team. It is a table that includes team members as row headings as well as decisions or deliverables as the column headings.

Action item

A result that an **owner** is accountable for delivering by a **deadline**. A completely specified action item must have a deliverable, a single owner, and a committed completion date.

Blind spot

The DKDK issues and risks and other circumstances that the team is blind to and unable to act on. If a member knows about an issue, but the team is blind to it, one often describes the issue as being "swept under the rug." This type of willful blindness is a very common pitfall that RUF practices intend to quash.

Business measures

The commercial impact—costs and benefits—that the team expects the project results to yield to their organization. The reason why the organization agrees to fund the project. A section of the **project statement.**

Cause (of risk)

When articulating a risk, a fact, true at the present moment, that motivates the concern of the risk.

CEI form

How risks are articulated in RUF by explicitly breaking the risk into its cause, effect, and impact.

COBL

see **Cost of being late.**

Commitment

"It will be so, even in the face of circumstances." Has the accountable owner of a result declared that she agrees to be counted on to make it so? We clearly distinguish when we have decided that something will be so, not as in "We'll try," but as in "We'll handle it."

Commitment phase

The time period on a project that begins with a decision to define a project and ends with an identified **project team** committed to achieve the project results.

Complaint

A description of something you think is wrong, told to someone who can't or won't do anything about it. Worries that don't lead to action.

Components

The list of actual things that will be built or created over the course of a project. A section of the **project statement**.

Concurrent and iterative

An essential feature of getting to **commitment:** you don't settle each axis of the **5W tradeoff** in sequence. Aspects of all of them get proposed, contradictions and risks are discovered, adjustments are made, the team iterates over drafts of all the **project documents** concurrently, evolving them from **draft** to **final**.

Core team

The subset of the **project team** that is required at all weekly accountability meetings and definition meetings. It is composed of individuals who can speak to "90 percent of the deliverables and 90 percent of the risks and issues" on the project. Every **track leader** is on the core team.

Cost of being late

A description, crafted during **project definition**, that identifies what would be the impact to the **business measures** if the project does not achieve its customer measures of success by the completion date or by important dates thereafter.

Cross-functional (team)

Participation that covers all areas of your project, crossing organizational boundaries and silos. Project leaders will include representatives from functional services (e.g., QA, support, legal) into the **core team**. Making your teams cross-functional from the beginning of your project is a core tenet of Risk Up Front.

Current (document)

Some documents evolve from draft to final, after which they serve as a reference. Other documents and tools (such as the RAP sheet and the **weekly schedule**) are to be kept up to date throughout the project. The most recently up-to-date version of a document is described as "current as of [date]."

Customer measures of success

What will be so in order that the project be considered a success from the point of view of the target customer. Typically described as capabilities that do not exist now but will exist upon successful completion of the project. How the target customer will measure the success of the project.

D

Deadline

The time by which a result is committed to be done.

Decision

A transparent choice to allocate resources to achieve a particular result.

Delivery phase

Once the team has committed to a project definition, the delivery phase begins. In this phase, the team does the work necessary to achieve the project's measures of success, by the committed end date.

DKDK

"Don't know you don't know." The things team members don't know, and they don't even know that they don't know them. These are the issues and circumstances in the team's **blind spot**.

Done

Every result to which team members have committed is in one of two states: done or not done. Done means that the committed result is achieved. We consider that a **commitment** has been clearly articulated if, when its deadline arrives, there is no argument as to whether it is done or not.

Draft (document)

A written proposal for decisions or results to which the team is not yet committed. In RUF, teams work collaboratively on drafts of key document to evolve them to their **final** state.

E

Effect (of risk)

A possible bad outcome. When articulating a risk in **CEI form**, the **effect** is the bad thing that might happen in the future if the risk were to materialize. As long as the risk exists on your project, the **effect** will not have happened yet—if it does, you no longer have a risk; you now have a problem.

End date

The date on which the project will end. During the **commitment phase**, the end date is tentative. During the **delivery phase**, the end date is **committed**.

Extended team

Members of the **project team** who are not part of the **core team**. These team members typically have fewer accountabilities or limited participation.

Facilitator

In a meeting, the individual accountable for chauffeuring the participants through the steps required to achieve its measures of success. For complex meetings, such as any DKDK meetings, the facilitator should be different from the meeting owner.

Final (document)

A document marked final should be understood to represent a **commitment**. See Draft (document).

Functional manager

The person within an organization who is accountable for providing people from a particular functional area to the projects that need it. They hire, train, manage, and support the people in their functional group. Functional managers are accountable for ensuring that their people are not overloaded and will be successful on the projects to which they have been assigned.

Ground rules

Agreed-upon accountabilities that apply to everyone on the team, such as "I am accountable for being on time to meetings." These often transcend a single project. For example, your organization may set ground rules (e.g., governance), and your project may be subject to ground rules set by external constraints (e.g., regulatory).

Impact (of risk)

In CEI form, the impact ties a particular risk to the success of your project. If a risk actually were to materialize, if the bad effect you feared actually were to happen, what would be the actual impact on your project? "Why would management care?"

Individual accountabilities

One of the RUF **project documents**. One page per team member that transparently answers the question, "What results, required by this project, can you count on me for?"

Integrity

"Do what you say." What a document claims to be so is in fact so. What a tool claims team members are committed to, they are actually committed to. It is the foundation of high-performance teams and must be measurable. Teams constantly assess where it is broken and fix it. We consider it to be the indispensable link between tools and results.

Levers of culture

The levers that you can control in order to change the culture of your team: **language**, **metrics**, **structures**, and **practices**.

Measure of success

An a priori description of a result in terms that are specific and measurable. Projects have **customer measures of success**, but the concept can be applied generally. For example, we recommend that a meeting invitation describe the measures of success for that meeting.

Milestone

In a schedule, a deadline at which a class of results are done or a gateway to a next phase can be passed. Milestones are recorded at key points in the **weekly schedule** for tracking by the team in the **WAM**.

Mitigation

An action item the team takes on in the name of reducing a risk.

N

Not done

See Done.

O

Opportunity

An idea for a value your team can create or a need your team can profitably fulfill. The seed of a potential **project**.

Opportunity sheet

A simple RUF form for collecting opportunities.

Optimistic procrastinator

The member of your team who assumes everything will go well, and if something might not go well, she'll deal with it later. We are all naturally optimistic procrastinators.

Owner

The team member who is accountable for causing the creation of a deliverable or some other result. This may or may not be the person who "does the work." It is the person who is on the hook to ensure the result gets done. We also refer to a meeting's owner, who is the team member who decides to call that meeting to solve a problem that she is on the hook to solve.

P

Practice

A structured meeting or other activity—a ritual—that happens on a regular basis or in response to a particular trigger. Practices are often DKDK activities and have a "just do it" quality.

Primary target customer

A target customer for whom we will change our project definition and product design to satisfy. See also **Secondary target customer.**

Priority (risk)

The ordering of risk, allowing the team to attack the most important risks first. In Risk Up Front, this ordering is based not on severity of impact but on how familiar and experienced the team is with the risk and its mitigation.

Project

An activity with a beginning, an end, and a measurable goal.

Project completion

A project is complete when the team has demonstrated that the customer measures of success on the **project statement** have been achieved—no sooner and no later.

Project definition

The description of the project in the form of its **5W trade-off**, resulting from the process of developing and committing a team to cause the results described by the structures developed during the **commitment phase**. This is what the **project team** is actually committing to deliver. It is articulated in the four RUF **project documents**.

Project leader
The individual accountable for the success of the project. The project's "prime mover." The **project leader** is ultimately accountable for causing all the activities that are necessary for that project's success.

Project statement
The RUF project document that is developed (starting from zero) during the **commitment phase** that articulates the **5W tradeoff** that the team has chosen.

Project team
The entire group of people who have accountabilities for delivering results required by a project. It includes both full-time and part-time contributors and all areas of the project. Related: core team, extended team, track leads.

Project week
RUF projects are run from the very beginning in weekly chunks, each culminating in a **weekly accountability meeting**. Each **WAM**, by reporting the team's weekly percent complete, measures the **integrity** of the commitments due during the preceding project week. Our recommendation is to start and end the project week in the middle of the work week, holding the **WAM** on, say, every Wednesday morning.

Q

Quality
Customer-perceived satisfaction.

R

RAP sheet
See **Risk action plan.**

Recorder (meeting)
The individual assigned to write down action items, risks, and edit project documents during a meeting. These documents are projected live so the meeting participants can see and respond to the recorded changes as they are made.

Resources
People, time, money, material—all are available in limited supply to your organization and to your project.

Result
A specific and measurable outcome that its owner, an accountable team member, will "cause to be so" by a deadline.

Risk
Something that might prevent a project from being successful.

Risk action plan (RAP sheet)
The RUF project document that articulates the risks of a project, including their current prioritization and mitigation activity, transparent to the team. The RAP sheet is kept current throughout the project.

Risk Up Front (RUF)
The practices, described in this book, used by teams to upgrade their operational performance and deliver projects faster and more reliably. These practices focus on tightening team **accountability, transparency, integrity,** and **commitment** as a means to push urgency and action around identifying and mitigating risk to the front of the project.

RUF project documents

RUF practices revolve around a small number of documents, the "four sheets of paper," that drive the conversations of **Risk Up Front**. These are the **project statement**, the team list with individual accountabilities, the **weekly schedule**, and the **risk action plan**.

Secondary target customer

A target customer for whom we will not alter our project definition. Their satisfaction is not necessary for the project to achieve its business measures.

Specific and measurable

These are the key properties to look for in order to effectively describe a result. Your language is specific when you know it will be clear whether the actual outcome is an instance of the desired result or not. A description such as "It will smell good!" might be troublesome to measure, but teams, when pushed toward measurability, will get creative. Language such as "It will be fast!" is perhaps measurable—after all, we can measure speed—but it is not specific because we will likely argue whether an outcome is fast enough. Alternative language, such as "20 mph" or "1 second," would be specific. A description of a result is measurable if we will be able to design a test (or measurement) that tells us if we achieved it or not.

Starting from zero

The notion that a project begins when a team, presented with an opportunity, works to determine what the project is. Instead of being told what to build, the **project team** begins by collaboratively exploring what **5W tradeoff** makes sense.

Structures

Elements of the organization of the people, tools, and spaces used by your teams—for example, a **project leader**, a meeting facilitator, a meeting room, a test lab, a document server, a software repository, a video conferencing link. The decision to utilize a structure entails the allocation of resources (e.g., money).

Success

The result is done by its deadline. A project is successful if it has achieved its customer measures of success by its completion date.

T

Target customer

The recipient who needs to be satisfied by the results of the project in order for your organization to realize the business results. One of the five required sections on the **project statement**. See Primary target customer and Secondary target customer.

Team

In RUF, this refers to the **project team** for a project.

Team list

One of the RUF **project documents**. If you are on the team list, you are on the team. If you are not, you are not. The **integrity** of the team list is critical to the early identification and mitigation of risk.

Time box

A **project definition** strategy that focuses on defining your project scope given a fixed project duration, rather than estimating your end date given a scope. It starts with the question, "What is a reasonable amount of time to spend on this?" and then considers the question, "What is the most useful thing to accomplish in the budgeted time?"

Track

The various subareas of the organization that have different kinds of expertise. Different kinds of projects require different tracks. Engineering, testing, marketing, sales, legal, manufacturing, operations, and customer support are all examples of tracks. In RUF, tracks are important because they must all be represented on the **project team**, and no track should go through more than two or three project weeks without some committed deliverable. Each activity on a project belongs within one of its track.

Track leader

The team member who is the accountable **owner** of a particular **track**. Every track leader is on the core team.

Transparency

"Team-wide clarity of what is so." Is the description of that committed result unambiguous throughout the team? Is there any argument about what the required result is? Is everyone aware of the actual state of the project? Team members give themselves both permission and the obligation to over-communicate rather than hide plans, outcomes, issues, and risks.

W

WAM

See **Weekly accountability meeting.**

Weekly accountability meeting

A RUF practice. A focused weekly meeting of the team, whose measure of success is to set the team up for 100 percent complete at its next **WAM.**

Weekly deliverable

Out of all the action items that arise over the definition and delivery phases of the project, the team will identify the results that need to be achieved by their respective deadlines in order to ensure the project succeeds. These action items are the weekly deliverables that get recorded in the **weekly schedule**. Some will be high-level milestones; some will be risky details.

Weekly percent complete

The fraction of weekly deliverables, committed to be done by the team within a project week that are in fact done. This number is reported and recorded in every **WAM**. The weekly percent complete is a measurement of team performance. It is therefore measured at the team level, not for individuals.

Weekly schedule

One of the RUF **project documents**, a spreadsheet that contains the weekly deliverables for the project against which the team will hold itself accountable. The entirety of these deliverables across all tracks, delivered each week add up to the successful project.

Z

Zebra

Something has to start with Z.

Fig. 35: Zebra

RUF PROJECT DOCUMENT EXAMPLES

On the following pages, you will find examples of the RUF Project Documents mentioned in this book.

As you read the examples, remember that these documents all evolved over time. The team did not simply write them down in a meeting. The language you see now was drafted, reviewed, research was done, prototypes were built, risks were mitigated, tradeoffs were made.

The process for developing these documents, the iteration and improvement, involved conversations that forced the team to confront the risks that stood in their way. Occasionally, these conversations were heated. Teams using Risk Up Front are constantly looking at what they're communicating and how they can upgrade their language.

While you review these documents, recall the Risk Up Front questions for read-throughs (chapter 7):

1. Is it clear?
2. Is it accurate?
3. Does it belong here?

PROJECT STATEMENT

Here is a complete example of a project statement. In order to present it in this book, it is shown on 5 pages, but in a real project statement, it fits within the maximum page limit for a project statement, which is at most 3 pages (US Letter or A4).

PROJECT OLAF
Project Statement
Status: Draft v2 12-Jan-2018

ONE-LINER:

> The growth in adventure picnics—away from vehicles and power sources—creates a market in metropolitan areas for a portable combination refrigerator grill unit which will ship April 1, 2019, in time for next summer's vacation market.

TARGET CUSTOMER:

1. **Primary Customer (We will change design for them)**

   a. The Picnicker: Urban and suburban dwellers, twenty-five to sixty years old, who live in apartment buildings with shared socializing space. They go to public parks and beaches with limited access to power and water. Targeting middle- to upper-middle-income individuals relative to local cost of living, e.g., $75K–$175K annual gross income in New York City. They are single, partnered, or in small families (five or fewer members). They enjoy light cooking and entertaining.

---

2. **Secondary Customer (We will not change design for them):**

   a. Private home dwellers who like entertaining in their private backyard.
   b. Companies that need a light-usage mobile refrigerator at remote sites.

CUSTOMER MEASURES OF SUCCESS:

1. Refrigeration:

   a. Maintain 38° temperature for 3.2 gallons for four hours, with no external power source.
   b. Operating ambient temperate from 35° to 100° F.
   c. Flash cool a six-pack of beer cans in three to five minutes.

2. Cooking (with no external power source or gas):

   a. Ability to grill ten hamburgers or boil 2 liters liquid.

3. Power

   a. Can charge two cell phones.
   b. Unit power source can be fully recharged from any supported power intake source within 1 hour.
   c. Can "hot swap" power storage cells during operation.

4. Mobility

   a. Power-assisted movement. Twenty kilogram true weight feels like 5 kg when moving over sidewalk or grass at 8 kmh. Optional add-on for power assist on rough terrain/beaches for $50 average selling price (ASP).

5. Control application software

    a. Unit is Bluetooth enabled to communicate to phone app.

    b. Ability to notify user of use conditions, beer cooled, food cooked, and system notifications, e.g., power low, fully charged, wheels jammed.

    c. Ability to set time and temperature for cooking and cooling. Ability to lock/unlock unit.

    d. Automatic software update feature.

    e. Telemetry feedback to us regarding system use, wear, and failures.

    f. Industry standard encryption (https) on all communications.

    g. Runs on iPhone and Android devices

        i. Compatible with iPhone 7/Apple Watch V1 and later through hardware/OS releases current as of ship date.

        ii. Compatible with Android Oreo and later through hardware/OS releases current as of ship date.

        iii. See Device Compatibility Matrix in Test Plan for more detail.

6. $100 ASP for base unit on Amazon.com

7. Certified to be sold in the United States and Canada (not European Union!)

8. Two-year warranty

9. No assembly

10. Free shipping

BUSINESS MEASURES OF SUCCESS:

1. Ship date of April 1, 2019.

2. Forecast sixty thousand units sold and shipped in first year.

3. Forty percent landed cost margin by 2018Q4, 50 percent margin by 2019Q4.

4. Cost of being late:

   a. Linear: $2M/month in steady state.

   b. Nonlinear: First year unit forecast is lowered to $40K if ship date is after June 15 (we will miss summer sales), i.e., loss of $800K.

COMPONENTS:

1. Drive train
   a. Altamont #7653B electric motor

   b. Durasco 65C-4 adjustable transmission

   c. Two "never flat" (GY72 or equivalent) tires, both powered.

2. Power system
   a. Next-generation drive replaceable battery and charging system (110V, Solar, CU-57 DC Charger)

   b. Butterfly Ultra-Solar 50W system

3. Structure
   a. Dura plastic-insulated panels, 30" × 15" × 24"

   b. Bracing made from ultralight Dura plastic

4. Control system
   a. Modify existing "droid" boards version 3.21

   b. Cat bus version 4.5

   c. Environmental monitoring system

5. Control unit firmware

6. Apps published in Google Play Store and iTunes Store.

7. Distribution deals with Best Buy, Amazon, REI, and Raymour & Flanigan

8. Warranty repair relationships and spare part strategy

9. Industrial design approved by internal corporate design committee (CDC)

TEAM LIST

	A	B	C	D	E	F
1	Project Olaf	Team List		Current as of	4/25/18	
2						
3	Track	Team Member	Role	Location	E-Mail	Phone
4	Project	Katja Rogowski	Project Leader	Bldg 4	k.rog@acme.com	4-1738
5	Project	Arnold Yu	Admin	Bldg 4	a.yu@acme.com	4-2151
6	Engineering	Ichiko Hashimoto	Lead Architect	Bldg 4	l.hash@acme.com	4-8314
7	Engineering	Benoit Duplessy	Engineering	Bldg 4	b.dup@acme.com	4-5782
8	Engineering	Harley Smith	Engineering/Materials	Bldg 4	h.smi@acme.com	4-9131
9	Marketing	Jane Hashimoto	Product Manager	Bldg 1	j.has@acme.com	1-9241
10	Marketing	Paul Houston	Marketing research	Bldg 1	p.hou@acme.com	1-2046
11	Sales	Tina Volare	Sales liason	Bldg 1	t.vol@acme.com	1-1762
12	Support	Ed Simpson	Customer Support Liason	Bldg 1	e.sim@acme.com	1-5242
13	Manufacturing	Pramila Adupal	Manufacturing Liason	Bldg 4	p.adu@acme.com	4-3378
14	Management	Beatrice Stein	General Manager	Bldg 1	b.ste@acme.com	1-1021

A spreadsheet that communicates who is on the team, what their roles are, and how to contact them. Super simple, but the value lies in keeping it in **integrity** over the life of the project. If you're on the list, you're on the team. If you're not, you're not.

Notice that we always put the state of the document at the top of every document. In this example, the state is "Current as of 4/25/18."

As this gets printed out and passed around, there is no question as to which version of the document people are referring to.

As an aside, many teams stamp "Last modified..." on their documents. "Current as of" makes a stronger statement—the document not only was updated on that date, but it was also "in integrity" on that date. The team represented on the list was the team in reality.

INDIVIDUAL ACCOUNTABILITIES DOCUMENT

PROJECT OLAF
Individual Accountabilities (IAs)

Team Member: Jane Hashimoto
Status: Final, signed off January 19, 2018
Role on Project: Product Manager

For this project, you can count on me for:

1. Getting customer information, including:

    a. Customer's process qualification plan

    b. Timeline and milestones from customer project and product release road map

    c. Any customer feedback required

2. Business outlook, forecast of adoption and production ramp, cost of being late

3. Negotiation of commercial and technical terms

4. Target customers definition

5. Approval of use cases for test plans, and Device Compatibility Matrix

6. Alignment of "look and feel" with rest of product line

7. Development, resourcing, and execution of product release plan

8. Assist project leader in getting executive sponsorship for the project

Known risks to my participation:

1. Cause: Product manager is only temporary on the project.
   Effect: We will have to revisit the project statement.
   Impact: Schedule will slip.

2. Cause: I am managing two other projects.
   Effect: It will take longer to complete commitment phase; issues will get missed.
   Impact: Delay in establishing committed end date of project.

Three-way review meeting completed and signed off by:

Team Member (taking on IAs):
Jane Hashimoto

Manager (allocating resource to project):
Anil Jayapal

Project Leader (IAs are necessary and sufficient):
Katja Rogowski

	A	B	C	D	E	F	G
1	Project Olaf	Weekly Schedule					
2		WAM Date	2/14/18				
		Percent Complete	89%		Goal: 100% by WAM Date		
3							
4	Track	Deliverable	Owner	Due	Status	Notes	
5	Project	Schedule next Definition Meeting	Katja	2/13/18	done		
6	Marketing	Draft, review, and signoff individual Accountabilities document	Jane	2/10/18	done	Set up review meeting with Katja and Anil	
7	Marketing	Draft "target customer" for Project Statement; Project statement updated.	Paul	2/13/18	done	Run by Jane before sending to Katja.	
8	Marketing	T-shirts design finalized and ordered	Jane	2/8/18	done	Tell Katja when they'll arrive	
9	Engineering	Pick vendor for insulation material	Benoit	2/13/18	done	Let Harley know	
10	Engineering	Order prototype parts	Harley	2/13/18	not done	needs Ichiko signoff; new date 2/20	
11	Engineering	Draft test plan complete, review scheduled.			done		
12	Engineering	Collect manufacturing integration requirements; Update spec.	Ichiko	2/10/18	done	with Pramila.	
13	Sales	Draft customer survey; publish to team for feedback.	Tina	2/13/18	done	deliver and analyze by 3/28	
14							
15							

Here is an example of the **weekly schedule** for Project Olaf, as it might appear while you are reviewing it at a **weekly accountability meeting**.

The weekly schedule consists of a workbook containing one spreadsheet tab for each **project week**. On Project Olaf, the project week ends every Wednesday, when the WAM is held.

Each tab contains the deliverables that are due by the date of the WAM, one row per deliverable.

The **weekly percent complete** is calculated automatically based on what is marked **done** and what is marked **not done**. Katja, the project leader, made sure she had this information prior to the **WAM**—she knows better than to waste time figuring it out in the room.

The example shows how the schedule might look on February 14, 2018. Almost everything was done, and the weekly percent complete is 89 percent. The team discussed the consequences of this and determined Harley could deliver it a few days later without impacting the overall schedule. Katja then copied and pasted the deliverable onto the tab for the following week.

RISK ACTION PLAN

Each row in the **risk action plan** spreadsheet represents one risk. Here are three risks taken from the RAP sheet for Project Olaf:

	A	B	C	D	E	F	G	H
1	Risk Action Plan	Project Olaf		Current as of		4/3/18		
2								
3	Track	ID	Cause	Effect	Impact	Priority	Owner	Proposed Mitigations
4	Marketing	1	Business plan does not include warranty forecast.	We may under-invest in product reliability. The failure rate may be too high.	Margins will be too low and product will be unprofitable. We may lose customers because of failure rate and repair cost.	High	Jane	1. Develop warranty cost model 2. Calculate MTBF for high cost items early 3. Consult with warranty cost experts 4. Do audit and "lessons learned" review on existing products 5. Budget an extra reserve for first year warranty costs.
5	Engineering	2	Prototype batteries explode at 30ºC in preliminary testing.	Exploding issue may take more time to resolve than planned, or may never work.	Schedule will slip. Won't hit battery specs. More expensive cost of goods.	Super High	Harley	1. Hold additional battery design review ASAP. 2. Fund parallel battery backup plan. 3. Order twice the number of prototypes. 4. Hire battery consultant. 5. Partner with battery supplier.
6	Project Mgmt	3	Individual Accountabilities have not been reviewed.	We may uncover resourcing issues late in the project.	Late schedule slip.	Medium	Katja	1. Complete IA reviews. 2. Bring IA's to scheduling meetings. 3. Hold IA reviews all on one day. 4. Add IA's to HR review process. 5. Have a team meeting with pizza focused on getting IA's committed.

Risk 1:

Track and ID	Marketing 1
Cause	Business plan does not include warranty forecast.
Effect	We may underinvest in product reliability. The failure rate may be too high.
Impact	Margins will be too low and product will be unprofitable. We may lose customers because of failure rate and repair cost.
Priority	High
Owner	Jane

Proposed Mitigations

1. Develop warranty cost model.

2. Calculate MTBF for high-cost items early.

3. Consult with warranty cost experts.

4. Do audit and "lessons learned" review on existing products.

5. Budget an extra reserve for first-year warranty costs.

Risk 2:

Track and ID	Engineering 2
Cause	Prototype batteries explode at 30°C in preliminary testing.
Effect	"Exploding issue" may take more time to resolve than planned, or may never work.
Impact	Schedule will slip. Won't hit battery specs. More expensive cost of goods.
Priority	Super-high
Owner	Harley

Proposed Mitigations

1. Hold additional battery design review ASAP.

2. Fund parallel battery backup plan.

3. Order twice the number of prototypes.

4. Hire battery consultant.

5. Partner with battery supplier.

Risk 3:

Track and ID	Project Management 3
Cause	Individual accountabilities have not been reviewed.

Effect	We may uncover resourcing issues late in the project.
Impact	Late schedule slip.
Priority	Medium
Owner	Katja

Proposed Mitigations

1. Complete IA reviews.
2. Bring IAs to scheduling meetings.
3. Hold IA reviews all on one day.
4. Add IAs to HR review process.
5. Have a team meeting with pizza focused on getting IAs committed.

ACCOUNTABILITY MATRIX

	A	B	C	D	E	F	G	H	I
1	Project Olaf	Accountability Matrix	Current as of	4/10/18		1=Owner			
2						2=Involved			
3	Team Member	Role	Propose Project Budget	Approve Budget	Design Prototype	Order Prototype Materials	Build Prototype	...	Alpha Party
4	Katja	Project Leader	1	2					1
5	Ichiko	Lead Architect			1	2	2		
6	Benoit	Engineering			2		1		
7	Harley	Engineering			2	1	2		2
8	Jane	Marketing	2						
9	Pramila	Manufacturing			2		2		2
10	Beatrice	General Manager		1					

Each row of the accountability matrix spreadsheet represents a team member, and each column represents a key **decision** or **deliverable** the project requires.

Put a "1" in a cell to indicate that the given team member is the **owner** for that deliverable. Put a "2" in the cell to indicate that the team member is involved in making the deliverable.

This means for every column, there should be only one owner ("1"), but there may be any number of other people involved ("2").

Such a spreadsheet quickly sorts out any confusion about ownership, where you discover a column has either no owners or more than one owner. It also quickly communicates to the team who is involved in key decisions or deliverables. The accountability matrix can also provide hints that a team member may be overloaded.

We suggest you develop an accountability matrix that sorts

out and communicates the key deliverables at the top level of the project. A typical accountability matrix at this level has ten to fifteen columns representing decisions, deliverables, or areas of accountability.

In areas of the project where accountabilities are complex or unclear, it is useful to create separate, more detailed accountability matrices to resolve those issues.

OPPORTUNITY SHEET

A simple form that some teams use to collect and organize ideas for future projects. The important point is to capture and communicate key aspects of the why and what that the submitter knows about on a single page.

Project Opportunity

Date: 7/25/2016

Submitter: Benoit@sales.newco.com

Opportunity: Sell plugin upgrades to base system to interoperate with database system X.

Target Customer: Acme Widgets and similar

Notes: Acme, along with at least three more of our largest clients, will be moving to system X in the next six months. This will be an easy upsell.

PROJECT PORTFOLIO SPREADSHEET

	A	B	C	D	E	F	G	H
1	Acme/Refrigerators	Project Portfolio Spreadsheet			Current as of:	4/25/18		
2								
3	Project Name	One-liner	Active	Project State	Owner	Start Date	End Date	Budget Notes
4	Frosty	Model 3.0 of our best-selling refrigerator, ChillMax. Incorporates internet	no	Completed	Jane Hashimoto	Actual: 10/4/17	Actual: 3/30/18	10 FTE, $2M, on budget.
5	Olaf	The growth in adventure picnics – away from vehicles and power sources – creates a market in metropolitan areas for a portable combination refrigerator grill unit which will ship April 1, 2017 in time	yes	Delivery Phase	Katja Rogowski	Actual: 1/12/2018	Target: 7/1/2019	15 FTE, $7M
6	Icecastle	ChillMax Model 3.1, with integrated inventory mgmt.	no	Budgeted	Jane Hashimoto	Target: 6/1/18	Target: 8/31/18	6 FTE, $1M

The **project portfolio spreadsheet** communicates what projects are in progress and which are coming up in the future. It makes crystal clear which projects are active and which are inactive, and it also identifies which are funded.

Remember, "active" means that we are expending resources, time, and money on this project now.

INDEX

5W tradeoff, 23, 315

ABOUT THE AUTHORS

ADAM JOSEPHS is a founding partner at Celerity Consulting Group LLC. Celerity trains and coaches organizations all over the world on applying Risk Up Front to accelerate product development and organizational change. Before Celerity, he managed engineering projects and product organizations at Apple Computer, Microsoft and a variety of startups. Adam is an adjunct faculty member in entrepreneurship and strategy at the David Eccles School of Business at the University of Utah, and has taught these subjects at New York University, U.C. Berkeley, Singularity University, and many industry conferences. He is a graduate of Stanford University and Oxford University. Adam makes his home in New York City, where he plays rugby and board games. He is a passionate advocate for local animal rescues. *http://strayfromtheheart.org/*

BRAD RUBENSTEIN is a partner at Celerity Consulting Group LLC. Prior to joining Celerity, Brad was an early software designer and architect at Sun Microsystems, and later was a core strategist creating trading and risk management infrastructure at Goldman Sachs. He joined Celerity to apply his extensive experience leading project teams to further develop Risk Up Front. Brad remains involved in theater and the arts. He served as chairman of the New York Festival of Song, and he is an active producer of theater and film. Brad holds a Ph.D. in Computer Science from the University of California at Berkeley.

Made in the USA
Middletown, DE
22 August 2021

46677160R00224